GLOBALISATION

&

NATIONALISM

VS

PATRIOTISM

DS KARTIKA

UNIQCO BOOKS

DS KARTIKA

Also by DS Kartika

Religions in India, an omniscient point of view

The late night beggar

You fool, Your's faithfully -Life

"A Nation's greatness is measured by

how it treats its weakest members "

Mahatma Gandhi

PREFACE

Globalisation and Nationalism are two central phenomena of the modern world. It is important to analyses the relationship between nationalism and globalisation because of the varying opinions held in regard to what impact globalisation has had on the world, how did it influence nationalism so farand how Patriotism is getting re-defined in an age of globalisation and resurgence of Nationalism.

When globalisation began to accelerate in the 1990s, globalists rejoiced and predicted that globalism would eventually weaken nationalism and international organisations, particularly the UN, would become more powerful. However, such optimism has turned out to be a wishful thought .All the most powerful forces in business, technology and finance pushed for deeper international integration. New supranational organisations such as the World Trade Organisation, the G20 and the International Criminal Court were set up to handle the cross-border issues that proliferated in a globalised world. Meanwhile the European Union, an organisation in which countries pool sovereignty and forswear nationalism, set itself up as the political model for the 21st century.

The most widely identified point in history for globalisation is the industrial revolution.The increased flow of capital, technology ,people, and customs due to globalisation has placed the role of contemporary nationalism into question.

DS KARTIKA

Globalisation and nationalism have had a, largely contemporary ,rift due to the magnitude to which globalisation has occurred in the 21st century. Such increased globalisation has put into question what it means to be a citizen of a state, whether or not state's still have distinctive cultures, and to what extent distinct national borders are still relevant. It begins to bug the question as to whether nationalism has increased or decreased due to modern globalisation.

Globalisation's effects on national identity are widely disputed. While some regard globalisation as undermining national identity and increasing cosmopolitanism. Others argue that it works in the opposite direction, possibly even reinforcing national feelings in the form of a backlash.The third argument says that globalisation has increased the sense of nationalism in such a way that national extremism has emerged ,anyways extreme right wing nationalism is a political phenomenon rather than a mass movement, which was implemented by cultural authoritarianism.

However, globalisation and nationalism promoted each other indeed, as a result of back lash or otherwise. Therefore, both globalisation and nationalism can co-exist in harmony and benefit from each other , then the patriotism which is defined 'as love and admiration for one's own country for what it does and willingness to die to defend it ,if required ' will often be in conflict with nationalism ,which advocates 'love for country ,no matter what it does'.

A patriot may take a stand against certain forms of globalisation as well as extreme nationalism based on the issues pertaining to it and criticise. Globalists may ignore or rubbishes it and nationalist would consider it as disloyalty at the best and treason at worst, unfortunately even in democratic countries bringing the freedom of speech and intolerance to difference of opinion into the debate.

The former president of France, Charles de Gaulle, once said: Patriotism is when love of your own people comes first. Nationalism is when hate for people other than your own comes first.George Orwell wrote that "nationalism is not to be confused with patriotism". For Orwell "patriotism is, of its nature, defensive, both militarily and culturally. Nationalism, on the other hand, is inseparable from the desire for power"

If you want to understand why nationalism and right-wing populism have grown so strong so quickly, you must start by looking at the actions of the globalists. In a sense, the globalists "started it." They initiated the chain of events which have caused right-wing nationalist reactions in many countries. This is consistent with scholarship suggesting that conservative movements are usually best understood as reactions to the waves of change promoted by progressives.

This book analyses the theories of leading international scholars and examine the effects of globalisation , impact of nationalism, ethics of patriotism ,all sort of extremism and disparity in an age of globalisation and resurgence of nationalism.

GLOBALISATION

GLOBALISATION

Globalisation is a process of interaction and integration among the people, companies, and governments of different countries . A process driven by international trade and investment and aided by information technology.Globalisation has grown due to advances in transportation and communication technology. With increased global interactions comes the growth of international trade, ideas, and culture. Globalisation is primarily an economic process of interaction and integration that's associated with social and cultural aspects. However, conflicts and diplomacy are also large parts of the history of globalisation, and modern globalisation

The term globalisation derives from the word globalise, which refers to the emergence of an international network of economic systems.One of the earliest known usages of the term as a noun was in a 1930 publication entitled Towards New Education, where it denoted a holistic view of human experience in education. The term 'globalisation' had been used in its economic sense at least as early as 1981, and in other senses since at least as early as 1944.Theodore Levitt is credited with popularising the term and bringing it into the mainstream business audience in the later half of the 1980s. Since its inception, the concept of globalisation has inspired competing definitions and interpretations. Its antecedents date back to the great movements of trade and empire across Asia and the Indian Ocean from the 15th century onward.Due to the complexity of the concept, various research projects, articles, and discussions often stay focused on a single aspect of globalisation

Sociologists Martin Albrow and Elizabeth King define globalisation as "all those processes by which the people of the world are incorporated into a single world society."

Economically, globalisation involves goods and services, and the economic resources of capital, technology, and data

Though many scholars place the origins of globalisation in modern times, others trace its history long before the European Age of Discovery and voyages to the New World, some even to the third millennium BC. Large-scale globalisation began in the 1820s.In the late 19th century and early 20th century, the connectivity of the world's economies and cultures grew very quickly. The term globalisation is recent, only establishing its current meaning in the 1970s.

In 2000, the International Monetary Fund (IMF) identified four basic aspects of globalisation: trade and transactions, capital and investment movements, migration and movement of people, and the dissemination of knowledge.Further, environmental challenges such as global warming, cross-boundary water, air pollution, and over-fishing of the ocean are linked with globalisation. Globalising processes affect and are affected by business and work organisation, economics, socio-cultural resources, and the natural environment. Academic literature commonly subdivides marketisation into three major areas: economic globalisation, cultural globalisation, and political globalisation.

GLOBALISATION & NATIONALISM VS PATRIOTISM

Economic Globalisation

Economic globalisation refers to the mobility of people, capital, technology, goods and services internationally. It is also about how integrated countries are in the global economy. It refers to how interdependent different countries and regions have become across the world. In the eighteen hundreds in the world economy generally, people and capital

crossed borders with ease, but not goods. In this century, people do not cross borders easily, but technologies, capital and goods do.Globalisation is a broad set of processes concerning multiple networks of economic, political, and cultural interchange, contemporary economic globalisation is propelled by the rapid growing significance of information in all types of productive activities and marketisation and by developments in science and technology.

Economic globalisation primarily comprises the globalisation of production, finance, markets, technology, organisational regimes, institutions, corporations, and labour.While economic globalisation has been expanding since the emergence of trans-national trade, it has grown at an increased rate due to an increase in communication and technological advances under the framework of General Agreement on Tariffs and Trade (GAAT

)and World Trade Organization, which made countries gradually cut down trade barriers and open up their current accounts and capital accounts.This recent boom has been largely supported by developed economies integrating with majority world through foreign direct investment and lowering costs of doing business, the reduction of trade barriers, and in many cases cross border migration.While GAAT opened up to the free movement of capital, goods and services and labour , The North American Free Trade Agreement (NAFTA) Opened up free movement of goods and services but not labour ..

Globalization radically increased incomes and economic growth in developing countries and lowered consumer prices in developed countries, it also changes the power balance between developing and developed countries and affected the culture of every countries opened up to it.

According to United Nations "Economic globalisation refers to the increasing interdependence of world economies as a result of the growing scale of cross-border trade of commodities and services, flow of international capital and wide and rapid spread of technologies. It reflects the continuing expansion and mutual integration of market frontiers, and is an irreversible trend for the economic development in the whole world at the turn of the millennium."The United Nations says the fast globalisation of the world's economies over recent decades is mainly due to the rapid development of science and technologies. They have created an environment in which the market economic system can spread across frontiers.

For example, the Internet and electronic communications today mean that businesses can employ workers from virtually anywhere in the world, and can trade in several countries at the same time without having to physically open up branches there.

As the world has become more economically globalised, so has the income and wealth inequality within countries. Some people believe globalisation is the cause – this has so far been difficult to prove.They argue that if companies have access to the whole world market, and most of those companies are located in a few countries – the US, EU and Japan – they will suck money out of the whole world in much greater quantities than if they sold just within their own markets.

The counter-argument is that globalisation brings well-paid jobs (compared to local pay rates) to emerging economies. A Ford factory worker in Mexico earns more and has better workplace conditions than he would as a farm labourer..

When looking at inequality between nations, however, globalisation has coincided with more equality between the advanced and emerging economies. The rich countries today represent a smaller percentage of global GDP compared to twenty or thirty years ago. Wealth inequality is not only a problem within emerging and low-income nations – it is also increasing in the advanced economies.

However ,globalisation has become a necessity in today's world due to its impact on the developing and developed countries. There is much access to developed countries resulting in easy technology transfer which in-turn resulting in higher productivity and easily available goods and services raised the living standards of people. It provides greater opportunities for those who have to access larger markets around the world. Cheap imports, more technology is available and increased capital flows are experienced by the countries involved in the global markets. They need to cope with certain policies created by the international policy makers like WTO, EEC etc.

Cultural Globalisation

Cultural globalisation refers to the rapid movement of ideas, attitudes, meanings, values and cultural products across national borders. It refers specifically to idea that there is now a global and common mono-culture – transmitted and reinforced by the internet, popular entertainment transnational marketing of particular brands and international tourism – that transcends local cultural traditions and lifestyles, and that shapes the perceptions, aspirations, tastes and everyday activities of people wherever they may live in the world'

Migration is an important aspect of cultural globalisation, and in this sense, this process has been going on for several centuries, with languages, religious beliefs, and values being spread by military conquest, missionary work, and trade. However, in the last 30 years, the process of cultural globalisation has dramatically intensified due technological advances in both transportation and communications technology.

The globalisation of food is one of the most obvious examples of cultural globalisation – food consumption is an important aspect of culture and most societies around the world have diets that are unique to them, however the cultural globalisation of food has been promoted by fast food giants such as McDonald's, Coca-Cola and Starbucks. The spread of these global food corporations has arguably led to the decline of local diets and eating traditions.

The Globalisation of sports is another fairly obvious example of cultural globalisation – think of all the international sporting events that take place – most notably the World Cup and The Olympics, and Formula 1, which bind millions together in a shared, truly global, 'leisure experience'.

Converging Global Consumption Patterns – today you can go to pretty much any major city in the world and share in a similar 'consumption experience'. Also, more and more people in Asia and South-America are coming to enjoy high-consumption lifestyles like in the West – car ownership and tourism are both on the increase globally for example. Central to this is the growth of similar styles of shopping malls, and leisure parks which provide a homogeneous cultural experience in different regions across the world.

.

Individuals and families are now more directly plugged into news from the outside world – some of the most gripping events of the past decade have unfolded in real time in front of a global audience. According to Giddens this means that more and more people have a more 'global outlook' and increasingly identify with a global audience – for example, television reporting of natural disasters in developing countries result in people in wealthier countries donating money to assist with relief efforts.

Giddens developed the concept of 'Cosmopolitanism' to describe this process of an emerging global identity.A criticism of Giddens is that some people perceive increasing globalisation as a threat to their ways of life and retreat into Fundamentalism and Nationalism as a defensive response, suggesting that Globalisation could go into reverse. In his classic 1999 text, Runaway World, Anthony Giddens argues that one consequence of globalization as de-traditionalisation, where people questions their traditional beliefs about religions, marriage, and gender roles and so on. He uses the concept of 'de-traditionalisation' rather than 'decline of tradition' to reflect the fact that in many cases people continue with their traditional ways of life, rather than actually changing them, but the very fact that they are now actively questioning aspects of their lives means cultures are much less stable and less predictable than before globalisation, because more people are aware of the fact that there are alternative ways of doing things and that they can change their way of life and traditions if they want to.The above processes are related to growth of urbanisation, especially the growth of global cities which have highly educated, politically engaged middle classes.

Ulrich Beck argues that a fundamental feature of globalisation is the development of a global risk consciousness, which emerges due to shared global problems which threatens people in multiple countries – examples include the threat of terrorism, international nuclear war, the threat of global pandemics, the rise of organised crime funded primarily through international drug trafficking, and the threat of planetary melt-down due to global warming.

On the downside, the constant media focus on such global problems has led to a widespread culture of fear and increasing anxiety across the globe, which has arguably contributed to things such as Paranoid Parenting and Brexit, but on the plus side, new global international movements and agencies have emerged through which people come together across borders to tackle such problems.

GLOBALISATION & NATIONALISM VS PATRIOTISM

Political Globalisation

Political globalisation refers to the growth of the worldwide political system, both in size and complexity. That system includes national governments, their governmental and intergovernmental organisations as well as government-independent elements of global civil society such as international non-governmental organisations and social movement organisations. One of the key aspects of the political globalisation is the declining importance of the nation-state and the rise of other actors on the political scene. The creation and existence of the United Nations has been called one of the classic examples of political globalisation

William R. Thompson has defined it as "the expansion of a global political system, and its institutions, in which inter-regional transactions (including, but certainly not limited to trade) are managed".Valentine M. Moghadam defined it as "an increasing trend toward multilateralism (in which the United Nations plays a key role), toward an emerging 'transnational state apparatus,' and toward the emergence of national and international nongovernmental organisations that act as watchdogs over governments and have increased their activities and influence". Manfred B. Steger in turn wrote that it "refers to the intensification and expansion of political interrelations across the globe". The longer definition by Colin Crouch goes as follows: "Political globalisation refers to the growing power of institutions of global governance such as the World Bank, the International Monetary Fund (IMF) and the World Trade Organization (WTO). But it also refers to the spread and influence of international non-governmental organisations, social movement organisations and transnational advocacy networks operating across borders and constituting a kind of global civil society." Finally, Gerard Delanty and Chris Rumford define it as "a tension between three processes which interact to produce the complex field of global politics: global geopolitics, global normative culture and polycentric networks."

PRACTICE

Salvatore Babones comprehended sources used by scholars for studying political globalisation and noted the usefulness of Europa World Year Book for data on diplomatic relationships between countries ,Publications of International Institute for Strategic Studies such as The Military Balance for matters of military, and US government publication Patterns of Global Terrorism for matters of terrorism.

Political globalisation is measured by aggregating and weighting data on the number of embassies and high commissioners in a country, the number of the country's membership in international organisation, its participation in the UN peacekeeping missions, and the number of international treaties signed by said country and the aspects of globalisation itself.

Political globalisation has several dimensions and lends itself to a number of interpretations. It has been discussed in the context of new emancipatory possibilities, as well as in the context of loss of autonomy and fragmentation of the social world.Political globalisation can be seen in changes such as democratization of the world, creation of the global civil society, and moving beyond the centrality of the nation-state, particularly as the sole actor in the field of politics. Some of the questions central to the discussion of the political globalisation are related to the future of the nation-state, whether its importance is diminishing and what are the causes for those changes; and understanding the emergence of the concept of global governance.

The creation and existence of the United Nations has been called one of the classic examples of political globalisation. Political actions by non-governmental organisations and social movements, concerned about various topics such as environmental protection, is another example.David Held has proposed that continuing political globalisation may lead to the creation of a world government-like cosmopolitan democracy, though this vision has also been criticised as too idealistic.

There is a heated debate over Political Globalization and Nation State. The question arises whether or not political globalisation signifies the decline of the nation-state. Hyper globalists argue that globalisation has engulfed today's world in such a way that state boundaries are beginning to lose significance. However, most disregard this as naiveté, believing that the nation-state remains the supreme actor in international relations.

EFFECTS OF GLOBALISATION

Globalisation has brought positive as well as negative effects into the world.

Positive effects :

Globalisation has become new catch phrase in the world economy, dominating the globe since the 90's of the last century. With the increased reliance of the people on the private capital and resources, international organisations are playing an important role in the development of developing countries. Globalisation has brought up many opportunities resulting in increased productivity and increased flow of capital within the economy. It has also resulted in increased investment providing greater job opportunities which has improved standards of living for the people.

Negative effects :

Globalisation has also thrown open varied challenges such as inequality of purchasing across and within different nations resulting in a widening gap between rich and poor, exploitation of labor in the name of cheap labor, environmental de-regulation, lack of democratic accountability and environmental deregulation has spurt open worsening in the economic situation. Another negative aspect of globalisation was that a majority of third world countries stayed away from the entire limelight

BENEFITS OF GLOBALISATION

The benefits from globalisation can be cited in the context of economic globalisation:

1.Trade in Goods and Services :

International trade ensures the allocation of resources resulting in increased productivity. As the matter of fact, the trade barriers in developing economies only hinder growth. The developing economies can benefit if all the resources are utilised efficiently. This is where the importance of reducing the tariff and non-tariff barriers crop up.

2.Movement of Capital :

Production of the developing economy is increased due to flow of capital across the countries. The Foreign Direct Investment (FDI) plays an important role in the development of an economy. With increased FDI, there would be more investment and more saving of the people of developing country receiving FDI resulting in over all benefit of the society in the form of enhanced standards of living and high productivity.

3.The Flow of Finance

The capital market development is one of the major features of the process of globalisation. The flow of capital ensures technology transfer, production of locations receiving a comparative advantage and by large the global foreign exchange markets are improved. The flow of capital and proper allocation of resources across countries increases financial stability across the world.

4.Other Benefits:

Globalisation is advantageous for the developing/developed nations. Due to globalisation business markets boundaries in the world have ended; one can make his product available in any corner of the world. Countries opt for globalisation because of the reason which include increased competition, comparative advantage, economies of scale and access to a greater range of products and services . globalisation results in lower inflation rate which is favourable because with the increase in competition", the prices fall. Another possible benefit is faster technological and, productivity growth because increased international competition has obliged business generally to innovate more rapidly since the '70s.

In today's world, no country can survive without globalisation especially the developing countries. Organisations need to operate globally due to increased competition. Without international operations, the organisations cannot sustain in the market for a longer time. In the developing countries, globalisation is an important process due to the immense benefits provided. It helps in the over all economic growth of the country by the foreign investment triggering saving within the country which could be used in the other investment. Other benefits are also a part of globalisation which vitalises it role even more. So, globalisation is a step for developing countries in the run to become developed.

CAUSES OF GLOBALIZATION

There are a number of factors in terms of development enabled globalization and became the cause.

1. Improved Communications

The development of communication technologies such as internet, email and mobile phones have been vital to the growth of globalisation because they help MNCs to operate throughout the world. • The development of satellite TV channels such as Sky and CNN have also provided worldwide marketing avenues for the concept and products of globalisation.

2. Improved Transport

The development of refrigerated and container transport, bulk shipping and improved air transport has allowed the easy mass movement of goods throughout the world. This assists globalisation.

3. Free Trade Agreements

Multi National Companies and rich capitalist countries have always promoted global free trade as a way of increasing their own wealth and

4.Influences

International organisations such as the World Trade Organisation and the IMF also promote free trade.

4. Global Banking

Modern communication technologies allow vast amounts of capital to flow freely and instantly throughout the world. • The equivalent of up to $US1.3 trillion is traded each day through international stock exchanges in cities such as New York, London and Tokyo.

5. The Growth of MNC's

The rapid growth of big MNCs such as Microsoft, McDonalds and Nike is a cause as well as a consequence of globalisation. • The investment of MNCs in farms, mines and factories across the world is a major part of globalisation. • Globalisation allows MNCs to produce goods and services and to sell products on a massive scale throughout the world.

IMPACTS OF GLOBALISATION

Impact of globalization is huge on countries, especially on the developing countries in terms of every aspect of living and are both advantageous and disadvantageous

1. Changed Food Supply

Food supply is no longer tied to the seasons. We can buy food anywhere in the world at any time of the year.

2. Division of Labour

Because MNCs search for the cheapest locations to manufacture and assemble components, production processes may be moved from developed to developing countries where costs are lower.

3. Less Job Security

In the global economy jobs are becoming more temporary and insecure.A survey of American workers showed that people now hold 7 to 10 jobs over their working life.

4. Damage to the Environment

More trade means more transport which uses more fossil fuels and causes pollution.,Climate change is a serious threat to our future.

5. Cultural Impact

Websites such as YouTube connect people across the planet. As the world becomes more unified, diverse cultures are being ignored. MNCs can create a monoculture as they remove local competition and thereby force local firms to close. Replacing

6. Increase in Nationalism

People have begun to realizes that globalisation can be challenged by communities supporting each other in business and society and through public protest and political lobbying.

GLOBALISATION & NATIONALISM VS PATRIOTISM

Advantages of Globalisation

1. Globalisation helps to boost the long run average growth rate of the economy of countries through:

(a) Improvement in the allocative efficiency of resources;

(b) Increase in labour productivity and

(c) Reduction in capital-output ratio.

2.Globalisation paves the way for removing inefficiency in production system. Prolonged protective scenario in the absence of globalisation makes the production system careless about cost effectiveness which can be attained by following the policy of globalisation.

3.Globalisation attracts entry of foreign capital along with foreign updated technology which improves the quality of production.

4.Globalisation usually restructure production and trade pattern favouring labour-intensive goods and labour-intensive techniques as well as expansion of trade in services.

5.In a globalised scenario, domestic industries of developing country become conscious about price reduction and quality improvement to their products so as to face foreign competition.

6. Globalisation discourages uneconomic import substitution and favour cheaper imports of capital goods which reduces capital-output ratio in manufacturing industries. Cost effectiveness and price reduction of manufactured commodities will improve the terms of trade in favour of agriculture.

7.Globalisation facilitates consumer goods industries to expand faster to meet growing demand for these consumer goods which would result faster expansion of employment opportunities over a period of time. This would result trickle down effect to reduce the proportion of population living below the poverty line.

8. Globalisation enhances the efficiency of the banking insurance and financial sectors with the opening up to those areas to foreign capital, foreign banks and insurance companies.

Dis-Advantages of globalisation

Globalization has its disadvantages also.

The following are the disadvantages:

1.Globalisation paves the way for redistribution of economic power at the world level leading to domination by economically powerful nations over the poor nations.

2.Globalisation usually results greater increase in imports than increase in exports leading to growing trade deficit and balance of payments problem.

3.Although globalisation promote the idea that technological change and increase in productivity would lead to more jobs and higher wages but during the last few years, such technological changes occurring in some developing countries have resulted more loss of jobs than they have created leading to fall in employment growth rates.

4.Globalisation has alerted the village and small scale industries and sounded death-knell to it as they cannot withstand the competition arising from well organised Multi National Companies

DS KARTIKA

5. Globalisation has been showing down the process to poverty reduction in some developing and underdeveloped countries of the world and thereby enhances the problem of inequality.

6. Globalisation is also posing as a threat to agriculture in developing and underdeveloped countries of the world. As with the WTO trading provisions, agricultural commodities market of poor and developing countries will be flooded farm goods from countries at a rate much lower than that indigenous farm products leading to a death-blow to many farmers.

7.Implementation of globalisation principle becoming harder in many industrially developed democratic countries to ask its people to bear the

pains and uncertainties of structural adjustment with the hope of getting benefits in future.

57

Globalisation and The World

The purpose of this study was to examine the impact of globalisation on world society. Research indicates that in the past century there has been worldwide surge in economic growth and more people lifted out of poverty than in all human history. World poverty has fallen within past 30 years. Since 1970's the development in China and India has played a significant role in reduction of the world poverty. However, economic growth is unbalanced and uneven across the globe. The economic growth has been concentrated just in fifteen wealthy countries. Whereas, eighty-nine other countries represent 1.6 billion people or one quarter of the world population are economically worse off than they were ten or more years ago. Sub-Saharan Africa requires greater focus to deal with poverty.

The present uneven economic growth trend has widened the gap between the rich and poor countries. According to economic forecasts if the current pattern of uneven economic growth continues, the poorest countries of the world will grow even poorer while the richest countries will become even richer. Across the world inequality has affected disproportionately the children and women of poor countries.

The present global uneven economic growth has raised a question can this gap between the rich and poor nations will be narrowed rather than widened in the future? This question has made social scientists, policy makers, and global international institutions to rethink about the impact of globalisation and future of rich and poor countries. The impact of globalisation has created a need for global action and interconnectivity at international, national, and local levels to make a human and sustainable world society in the 21st century.

Since the mid-twentieth century globalisation has become a buzzword to talk about societies, and is defined as a way of integrating worldwide government policies, cultures, societies, social movements, financial markets through trade and exchange of ideas (Schaefer 2005). The process of globalisation has been accelerated by modern means of communication and transportation, and gives the image that the world is unified globally. It appears that in the 21st century globalisation is an unaltered way and will continue even though 75% of the world's population has access to daily television reception and only 20% has access to consumer cash or credit.

However, professionals have differences of opinion about globalisation and its effect. One group sees globalisation is a natural result of advances in communication technology, particularly the Internet and satellite transmission of mass media. Second group views it more critically and sees globalisation as an extensive movement of capitalism and related values and ideas among the nations of world . In fact globalisation has been underway for several hundred years. It started with colonialism which fuelled economic development of already wealthy countries by keeping the economies of the colonised countries under- developed.

In modern times powerful nations are rarely involved in conquest and subjugation of weak nations. Whereas, with the new forms of communication systems, Internet and transportation powerful nations are able to exploit weaker countries for their commercial gains. Powerful countries can use weaker countries as a source of cheap raw materials and cheap labor. Because of their access to better technology, wealthy nations are able to produce higher quality goods at lower price than the poor nations. This advantage allows them to have a more favourable balance of trade and ultimately gives them greater control of the world's financial resources, and widened inequality among the rich and poor nations . The following section will analyse the impact of globalisation on world society.

According to the United Nations Development Programme the gap between countries has widened, even though there has been worldwide surge in economic growth over the past decades, but it has benefited only a handful of countries. More specifically, the benefit of global economic growth has been concentrated in just fifteen countries. Whereas, eighty- nine other countries which represent 1.6 billion people or one quarter of the world population are economically worse off than they were ten or more years ago (United Nations Development Report). Out of these eighty-nine countries seventy are low income and developing countries. Their income level has fallen below those of the 1960's and 1970's. As a result, the poorest 20 percent of the world population saw their meagre share of global income cut nearly in half over the past three decades, while the richest 20 percent of the world's population increased their share of global income by 15 percent in the same period. In other words, the income share ratio of the world's richest and poorest people have doubled during this time; increasing from 30:1 to 61:1. The above findings lead to conclude that "in the past 15 years the world has become more economically polarised – both between countries and within countries. If the present trends continue, economic disparity between the industrial and developing nations will move from inequitable to inhuman"(U.N. Development Programme)

In global society nations have differing amounts of power and want to ensure that their interests are met. The developed and less developed countries of the world experience serious inequalities in wealth that have immediate consequences for their citizens. The low-income countries are poor because of the policies and practices and the high income countries pursue in order to mass a greater share of global wealth. Because of their policies and practices the low- income countries are in a position of relative dependency on high-income countries.

Powerful nations, like powerful ruling classes, seek to retain their favoured positions while keeping other nations in their place. In a global economy, such dominance is accomplished through financial pressure, such as powerful industrialised countries set world prices on certain goods, rather than use brute force . The economic base of poor countries is weak, therefore they often have to borrow money or buy manufactured goods on credit from wealthy countries.

The huge debt they build up to locks them into a downward spiral of exploitation and poverty. As a result, they cannot develop an independent economy of their own and thus remain dependent on wealthy ones for their very survival . In short, just as upper-class people can exploit and exercise power over lower-class people within a society similarly, wealthy countries can exploit poor countries in the global market place. In consequence of it the global economic gap has widened .

The average per capita yearly income in Western Europe, the United States, Canada, and Japan is about $22,000. In the less developed countries South America, Asia, and Africa it's a little over $300 . Thus, wealthy countries contributing 20% of the world's population accounts for 65% of the world's income. In contrast, less affluent developing countries account for 67% of the world's population but only 18% of its income.

Assets hold by the world's 200 wealthiest individuals total $ One-trillion, for an average of five billion each. After doubling since 1995, their total wealth equals' the combined annual income of the world's 2.5 billion poorest people, meanwhile eighty nations reported incomes lower than a decade age. Sixty countries have grown steady poorer since 1980. Three Billion people presently live on $2 or less per day while 1.3 billion get by on $1 or less .

The richest three individuals in the world have assets that exceed the gross domestic product of the 48 least developed countries "For instance, the 400 wealthiest U.S. citizens hold financial assets equivalent to one-eighth of the gross domestic product of the world's largest economy Their personal wealth grew by an average $940 million each from 1997 to 1999 – a per capita daily increase averaging $1,287,67 ($225,962 per hour). Eighty-six percent of stock market gains went to the top 10 percent of U.S. households while 42 percent of it went to the most well-to-do one percent"

Further eye-Opening Statistics reveals disparity between the over-consumption and under-consumption between the wealthy and poor countries

1.Wealthy countries consume 85% as the world's supply of paper, 79% of its steel, 80% of all commercial energy, and 45% of all meal and fish.

2..Grains fed to U.S. Livestock equal the amount of food consumed by the combined human populations of India and China.

3..A single child born in Western Europe, Japan, or the United States uses as much of the earth's resources as an entire village of African children.

4..Americans spend about $8 billion a year on cosmetics-$2 billion more than the estimated annual amount needed to provide basic education for everyone in the world.

5.Europeans spend about $2 billion a year or more on ice cream than the estimated amount needed to provide clean water and safe sewers for the world's population.

The gap in education and quality of life is particularly striking. Only about 20 percent of school-age children in poor countries enrolled in Secondary School compared to 90 percent in affluent countries. In wealthy countries 40 percent of college age people go to college; in poor countries only 30 percent do. The number of children die before the age of five is nearly 20 times higher the age of poor countries than in rich one . It is estimated that about 24 percent of the world's adult population is illiterate, of that 30 percent of the world's female adult population is illiterate. In low income countries the illiteracy rate for women is nearly 46 percent.

The gap in medication disturbing , a vast majority of HIV infected people around the world don't have access to the effective drug treatments that are available in the west. Consequently, the AIDS cases and AIDS deaths are dropping in Western Industrialised countries but are increasing dramatically in less developed countries. According to the United Nations, of the 26 million people worldwide infected with HIV virus, 30 million are poor by world standards, living on less than $2 a day. Impoverished countries in Sub-Saharan Africa, alone, account for 69% of the World's victims of HIV and AIDS. In Botswana and Zimbabwe, for instance, one in every four adults is infected. In some major cities, 50% women in prenatal clinics test positive for HIV . The death of infected africans are more than five times the number of AIDS-related deaths in the United States in the last two decades , and it is estimated that between one half and two thirds of the young adults in these African countries will eventually die of AIDS.

GLOBAL INEQUALITY

Trends in global inequality are found both between and within countries. Inequality between the countries has been characterised by two divergent trends in recent decades. The gap between the richest and the poorest countries over the past 40 years has been widened and a significant number of countries have fallen further behind compared not only to industrial countries but to other developing countries also. The income distribution between countries has consequently worsened. However, at the most populous ones, the gap between their average incomes and that of industrial countries has begun to narrow. Overall, inter-country inequality weighted by population has decreased as a result, China and India account for the bulk of this improvement while inter-country inequality has improved; however inequality within many of the most populous countries with a large number of poor has increased modestly (World Bank)

GLOBALISATION & NATIONALISM VS PATRIOTISM

ECONOMIC INEQUALITY AND POVERTY

The United Nations Development Programme created three basic minimal essential criteria which are essential for human requirements (to be well nourished, to be able to reproduce, and to be educated) to measure the poverty, which was defined as Capability Poverty. According to Capability Poverty as a measure, the number of people who are poor world wide increased from 1.3 billion (33 percent) to 1.6 billion (37 percent). Capability poverty appears to be most widespread in South Asia. In Africa, both income poverty and capability poverty are high. In contrast many countries in Latin America have done well in addressing capability poverty but income poverty remains severe. The global poverty is disproportionately found in the United States among women and children also .

GLOBALISATION & NATIONALISM VS PATRIOTISM

GENDER AND GLOBAL POVERTY

Few societies in the world treat women as well as men. Inequality between men and women are not necessarily less in high income countries, but in disadvantaged countries on global scale, women are likely to be even more disadvantaged. Women in these countries experience double deprivation. The deprivation of living in a poor country and depravation imposed because they are women. According to United Nations women represent 60 percent of world population and perform nearly two-thirds of all working hours, they receive only one-tenth of world income and own less than one percent of world property (United Nations)

Further, across the world women are more likely (than men) to be illiterate. It is estimated that 24 percent of the world's adult population is illiterate, of that 30 percent of the world's female adult population is illiterate. In low income countries the illiteracy rate for women is nearly 46 percent (United Nations Development Programme) Indeed in most countries throughout the world, women are the most disadvantaged of the disadvantaged.

CHILDREN AND GLOBAL POVERTY

The burden of poverty is spread unevenly throughout the world with population of low income countries suffering is far greater due to more severe poverty than other countries in the global stratification hierarchy. In low-income countries the poorest households tend to be those with the greatest number of children or economically dependent members (elderly or diseased people). Twenty five million children between the ages of five and fourteen are in the paid labor free in virtually in all countries, including United States, it is particularly prevalent in Asia, where 150 million children are in the labor force and in Africa where approximately 80 million children are working .

According to Development Specialist Susan George "Half of these millions of child labourers working in "outrageous conditions" are under 14 years old. The advantage for corporations is that they receive "three compliant and defenceless children for the price of one adult. The result of repression is to drive down wages and replace adults". For example in India, the numbers of working children.and jobless adults are roughly the same.

The practice of child labour perpetuates poverty. These children grow up to become the next generation of uneducated and untrained adults. With the World Trade Organization legislating for the rights' of corporations in the name of "free trade: nations are unable to prohibit child labour without violating international trade rules enforced by Western institutions The response of the Western Powers to this state of affairs is instructive. The U.S. Government for instance has resorted only to the insignificant public relations stunt of requesting companies to adopt a 'voluntary' code of conduct .

According to International Labor organisation children's work conditions are frequently exploitative and abusive. Work long hours in unhealthy environment for subsistence wages. In Pakistan, for example nearly 10,000 children under the age of fourteen work 10 hours a day hard-sticking leather soccer balls, for a daily wage of about $1.20 . Children beating, imprisonment, homeless, and abandonment by parents are common. Children of six years can be found on street. Nearly 13 million children on streets in Latin American countries. In most Latin American cities begging, selling sex or drugs or stealing is in order to survive. Children sleep on the sidewalks, in alley under bridges and even in sewer tunnels. In Brazil, several hundred street children are murdered each year by the police.

"The rise of global inequality and impoverishment within the current order has therefore been enormous, systematic and relentless. Western pro-corporate policies are however, domestic as well as international, resulting in the increase in domestic impoverishment and inequality. Thus, even within the richest countries inequalities have widened and poverty increased "

RESULTS OF GLOBALISATION

The evidence suggests that in the past century more advances have been seen in global prosperity and more people lifted out of poverty than in all human history. There are many reasons for this achievement, but globalisation has played an important catalytic role. World poverty has fallen dramatically in the past 50 years. For example, since 1970's the development in China and India has played a significant role in reduction of the world poverty. However, economic growth is not balanced across the globe. Some countries have witnessed tremendous growth and others have fallen in poverty. For example the Sub-Saharan Africa requires greater focus to deal with poverty . The present uneven economic growth trend has widened the gap between developed and developing countries.

According to economic forecasts if the current pattern of uneven economic growth continues, the poorest countries of the world will grow even poorer while the richest countries will become even richer. For example it is estimated that by 2030, global production will triple.

However in Sub-Sahara Africa, per capita income will fall to just $32 a year, whereas in high-income countries, average per- capita income will approach $40,000. Many of the countries of East Asia are expected to catch up to the high-income countries in terms of per-capita income. By 2050, china's per capita income is not likely to approach that level until at least 2080, and India's will not reach the $40,000 per capita mark until about 2130 the twenty second century . The present world unbalanced and uneven economic growth has raised a question can this gap between the rich and poor nations will be narrowed rather than widened in the future? This question has made professionals and global society to rethink about the impact globalisation and future of rich and poor countries .

EFFORTS TO NARROW THE GAP

A number of social scientists believe that it is possible to narrow the gap, but they stress that our goals must be reordered. Instead of concentrating on the rate of economic growth, social scientists and policy makers should pay more attention to the quality of economic growth. Economic growth for the human development, such as improvement in health and education; higher standards of living, and sustain natural resources, should be the priority if we want to avoid future world "gargantuan in its excesses grotesque in its human and economic inequalities" (United Nations Development Programme). If we continue to focus on the rate of economic growth only, we will likely to create a world where people will be "jobless, voiceless, rootless, futureless, and ruthless (United Nations Development Programme).

Ahmed, proposed that " the only real way to address the escalating social, economic and political problems faced by the majority of the world's population as a result of globalisation is to transfer the unjust structures responsible for these problems. The current world order is geared inherently to fulfil the interests of corporate elite based primarily in the West, directly at the expenses of the rights, and well-being of hundreds of millions of people around the world. Unless World order undergoes a meaningful and drastic transformation of structure the basis of a fundamental re-evaluation of values, ethics and world view, this order will continue to be increasingly engulfed by a crisis of its own making with devastating consequences".

A detailed World Bank study concluded that economic growth is crucial but often not sufficient to create conditions in which the world's poorest people can improve their lives. But we also recognised the fundamental role of institutions and social changes to strength the development processes and the inclusion of poor people. The study made recommendations that the developing countries, governments at all levels, donor countries, international agencies, N.G.O.'s, civil society, and local communities mobilise behind three priority areas:

1. Opportunity:

Expanding economic opportunity for poor people by stimulating economic growth, making markets work better for poor people and working for their inclusion, particularly by building up their assets, such as land and education .

2. Empowerment:

Strengthening the ability of poor people to shape decisions that affect their lives and removing discrimination based on gender, race, ethnically and social status

3. Security:

Reducing poor people's vulnerability to sickness, economic shocks, crop failure unemployment, natural disasters and violence and helping them cope when such misfortunes occur. Advances in these areas are complementary. Each is important in its own right and each enhances the others. These priorities can allow the poor to have greater independence and security in their day-to-day lives: for example:

(a) empowering women and other socially disadvantaged groups expand their range of economic opportunities, and

(b) strengthening poor people's organisations and their involvement in decision making processes enable them to press for improved services and for policy choices that respond to their needs. Finally, making poor people less vulnerable makes it easier for them to take advantage of potential market opportunities . These priorities can allow the poor to have greater independence and security in their day to day lives, and would create opportunities to participate in the market.

Further, World Bank in World Development Report 2003 made the following suggestions to work with the problem of the poverty which involves cooperation at local, national and international levels.

1. New alliances are needed at the local, national and global levels to better address the problem of poverty. The burden for development must be shared widely.

2. Rich countries must further open their markets and cut agricultural subsidies that deplete income in third world farmers, and they must increase the flow of aids, medicines, and new technologies to developing countries.

3. Governments in the developing world in turn must become more accountable and transparent, and ensure that poor people are able to obtain secure large tenure, as well as access to education, health care, and other basic services. The burden of

guaranteeing sustainable development must be shared locally, nationally, and globally.

4..Developing Countries need to promote participation and subscribe democracy; inclusiveness and transparency as they build the institutions, need to manage their resources.

5. Rich countries need to increase aid, cut poor country debts, their markets to developing countries exporters and help transfer technologies needed to prevent diseases, increase energy efficiency and bolster agricultural productivity.

6. Civil Society organisations contribute when they serve as a voice for dispersed interdependent provides independent verification of public, private and non-governmental performance.

7.Private firms contribute when they commit to sustainability in their daily operations, and create incentives to pursue their interests while advancing environmental and social objectives.

8.Lastly, the World Development Corporation (WDC) proposed a corporation of all multinational corporations to bring technology credit access to world markets and management know-how to improvised areas. Its projects would need to be subsidised at first but should become profitable in the long run. In addition, linking global corporations to local projects would create profitable endeavours in order to reduce poverty permanently and irreversibly.

SUMMERY

In sum, it can be concluded that globalisation has significantly improved the world economy, but due to unbalanced and uneven economic growth the world's social and poverty problems are magnified. The interconnectivity among world nations has created a need for a global collective action to combat the world poverty and create a humanitarian and sustainable global world in the 21st century. In order to make globalisation sustainable and viable requires focus from below which involves interdependence at the grassroots level that aims to protect, restore, and nurture the environment; to enhance ordinary people's access to the basic resources they need to live a dignified existence to democratise local, national, transnational political institutions, and to ease tensions and prevent violent conflict between power centres and authority structures

NATIONALISM

GLOBALISATION & NATIONALISM VS PATRIOTISM

NATIONALISM

Nationalism is the belief that a particular nation and its culture, people, and values are superior to those of other nations and that one's own nation will benefit from acting independently, rather than in coordination with other nations. It can also include the belief that a certain large social group of people deserves to have its own independent nation.

Nationalists are those people who identify, perhaps strongly, with a particular nation. Through nationalism, people show a strong loyalty and devotion to their existing nation or desired future nation that exceeds most other concerns. Nationalism influences people on a day-to-day basis and shapes their lives in various ways. Nationalism is often most strongly felt by groups that are seeking to establish a new nation.

Nationalist movements are efforts to establish or actively maintain a particular nation. Nationalists promote self-governance (freedom from foreign political control) of their nation to maintain independence from other nations. Nationalism often makes use of stereotypes (an oversimplified opinion of others based on limited information or exaggerated perceptions) to create and maintain a unity of prejudice against people of other nationalities or different set of beliefs or Ideology . Nationalism requires distinctions between Strong support for a particular nation and not other nations as much. The stereotypes are mostly negative and that may result in members of other nations becoming labeled as an enemy.

People who share common nationalistic attitudes often share some combination of a common language, culture, religion, or other social values. Often, new nations are established based on a certain ethnicity of the people or some other form of common identity such as religious affiliation. By the late twentieth century, ethnicity had become increasingly important over all other factors. As a result, people who are born into a particular ethnic group are also born into a nation or group seeking a nation of their ethnicity.Therefor membership in such nationalistic movement is often hereditary rather than chosen and are not based on citizenship. Nationalists draw strength and resources from people of same ethnicity spread across the glob to form a nation of their language , culture , religion or other social ethics in order to remain cohesive and distinguish themselves from members of other nations.

National symbols are adopted, a national culture is promoted, and folklore and mythology is used to justify the nation's existence and feelings of superiority ,in addition to that a national music, literature, sports, and eating habits are identified to help establish or maintain a national identity. Some nationalists may even promote a national religion and discourage the practice of other religions.Just as nationalism has greatly affected the course of world history throughout the past several centuries, it still has the capability to influence what can happen. Nationalism can lead to separatism (seeking to form a new nation from one currently existing), irredentism (reclaiming a lost homeland), or militarism (forceful expansion of a nation). Nationalism can stir intense emotions, and extreme forms of nationalism can lead to extensive violence, even ethnic cleansing (a planned attempt to eliminate a targeted ethnic group of people completely by killing all its members .

Definition of Nationalism

a sense of national consciousness exalting one nation above all others and placing primary emphasis on promotion of its culture and interests as opposed to those of other nations or supranational groups.

Nationalism is the desire for political independence of people who feel they are historically or culturally a separate group within a country.Historically, nationalism has been used to define and explain everything from radical political and militaristic movements like Nazism to strong protectionist policies controlling modern foreign policy and economy. While patriotism ,an easily confused term with nationalism, is perhaps harmless ike that exuded on the 4th of July, nationalism is more sinister in nature.

Nationalism centers on a country's culture, language, and often race. It may also include shared literature, sports, or the arts, but is primarily driven by cultural associations. And, it promotes the nation at the expense of others. Nationalist countries or leaders don't join international organisations or associations, and even if they do, maintain a superior view of themselves to the detriment of other nations.

Nationalism has a positive view of conquering other nations as it sees itself as the ultimate nation.

Any ideologies that undercut or contradict the nationalist ideas are opposed.Nationalism, in its extreme forms, has led to genocide, the Holocaust and more specifically, the ethnic cleansing in Bosnia in the 1990s. And the most recent one in Myanmar from 2016-2017

Nationalism is a kind of Devotion, mostly excessive devotion, to the interests or culture of a particular nation-state. The belief that nations will benefit from acting for it ,on its own rather than collectively, emphasising national goals rather than international goals.

Nationalism has long been ignored as a topic in political philosophy, written off as a relic from bygone times. It came into the focus of philosophical debate ,almost three decades ago, in the nineties, partly in consequence of rather spectacular and troubling nationalist clashes such as those in Rwanda, the former Yugoslavia and the former Soviet republics. Surges of nationalism tend to present a morally ambiguous, and for this reason often fascinating, picture. "National awakening" and struggles for political independence are often both heroic and cruel; the formation of a recognisable national state often responds to deep popular sentiment but sometimes yields inhuman consequences, from violent expulsion and "cleansing" of non-nationals to organised mass murder.

The moral debate on nationalism reflects a deep moral tension between solidarity with oppressed national groups on the one hand and repulsion in the face of crimes perpetrated in the name of nationalism on the other. Moreover, the issue of nationalism points to a wider domain of problems related to the treatment of ethnic and cultural differences within democratic polity, arguably among the most pressing problems of contemporary political theory.

In the last decade the focus of the debate about nationalism has shifted towards issues in international justice, probably in response to changes on the international scene. Bloody nationalist wars such as those in the former Yugoslavia have become less conspicuous, whereas the issues of terrorism, of the "clash of civilisations" and of hegemony in the international order have come to occupy public attention. One important link with earlier opinion is provided by the contrast between views of international justice based on the predominance of sovereign nation-states and more cosmopolitan views that insist upon limiting national sovereignty or even envisage its disappearance. Another new focus for philosophers is provided by issues of territory and territorial rights, which connect the topic of nation-states (or, "the nation state") with questions about boundaries, migration, resource rights and vital ecological matters.

Emergence of Modern Nationalism

Nationalism is a modern movement. Throughout history people have been attached to their native land and the traditions of their forefathers to establish territorial authorities but it was not until the end of the 18th century that nationalism began to be a generally recognised sentiment and movement moulding public and private life and as one of the important if not the greatest, single determining factors of modern history. Because of its dynamic vitality and its all-pervading character, nationalism is often thought to be very old ,sometimes it is mistakenly regarded as a permanent factor in political behaviour. Actually, the American and French revolutions may be regarded as its first powerful manifestations. After penetrating the new countries of Latin America ,it spread in the early 19th century to central Europe and from there, toward the middle of the century, to eastern and southeastern Europe. At the beginning of the 20th century nationalism flowered in the ancient lands of Asia and Africa. The 19th century has been called the age of nationalism in Europe, while the 20th century has witnessed the rise and struggle of powerful national movements throughout Asia and Africa.

Nationalism didn't arise until the seventeenth century. Before that, people focused on their local town, kingdom, or even religion. The nation-state began in 1658 with the Treaty of Westphalia. It ended the 30 Years War between the Holy Roman Empire and various German groups.

Industrialisation and capitalism strengthened the need for a self-governing nation to protect business rights, and merchants partnered with national governments to help them beat foreign competitors. The government supported this mercantilism because the merchants paid them in gold. The steam-powered printing press helped enable nations to promote unity within and prejudice against outsiders.

In the late 18th century, the American and French revolutions formalised large nations that were free of a monarchy. They ruled by democracy and endorsed capitalism. In 1871, Otto von Bismarck created the nation of Germany from different tribes. By the 20th century, the entire American and European continents were governed by sovereign nations.

The Great Depression created economic conditions so harsh that most countries adopted nationalism as a defence. Fascist leaders like Adolf Hitler in Germany and Benito Mussolini in Italy used nationalism to override individual self-interest, subjugating the welfare of the general population to achieve social goals.

Nationalism under fascism works within existing social structures, instead of destroying them. It focuses on "internal cleansing and external expansion," according to Professor Robert Paxton in "The Anatomy of Fascism." The thinking justifies violence as a way to rid society of minorities and opponents.

World War II convinced all the Allied nations to endorse global cooperation. The World Bank, the United Nations, and the World Trade Organisation were just three of many global groups endorsed it. In the 1990s, Europe's nations formed the European Union. Nationalism became dangerous, and globalism became salvation.

In the 21st century, nationalism returned after the Great Recession. In 2014, India elected Hindu nationalist Narendra Modi. In 2015, Vladimir Putin rallied Russians to invade Ukraine to "save" ethnic Russians. In 2016, the United Kingdom voted to Brexit, the British exit from the EU.

In 2016, the United States elected populist Donald Trump to the presidency. Trump's policies follow a type of "half-baked, spurious nationalism," according to Senator John McCain, R-AZ. Trump and his former adviser Steve Bannon advocate economic nationalism.

IDEOLOGY

Nationalism as an ideology, gives the nation a sense of unity by imposing the same set of identities on the people ,for instance linguistic, historical, cultural or even religion though thats the worst . Especially peculiar to nationalism is defining the nation against another inside or outside of the state borders.

However, this short definition by no means exhausts all the complexities of nationalism. So much so that some post-modern scholars insist on using the plural "nationalisms" to do justice to the whole spectrum of experiences. It matters, for instance, whether we are talking about a nationalism in 21st century or 19th-century Europe or a nationalism in post-World War I India.

Nationalist ideology continues to shape global politics today, and yet twenty-first-century nationalism is faced with a unique set of challenges. For example, migration and diaspora create cultural, economic and social networks which now bind people across entire continents, let alone countries. The much-discussed onset of globalisation, together with regional integration, has also pushed governments to revise their nation-building rhetoric. Some nation-builders have reacted to globalisation as a potential threat, while others see it as a significant boost to their country's power and influence. This is important because of the implications for nation-state authority and legitimacy; nation-states seek to square national autonomy with deep involvement in regional alliances, trading networks and international organisations. At the same time, sub-state nationalists continue to compete for people's loyalty and support. Today, nationalists must reconsider the meaning of self-determination, independence, autonomy and sovereignty in an increasingly interconnected world.

The end of the twentieth century saw the unfolding of various forms of transnationalism, which led some to predict the end of the nation-state, while a spike in ethnic conflict and secession following Cold War collapse led others to identify a new rise of nationalism. All manner of minority, sub-state, terrorist, democratic, irredentist and post-communist nationalisms have been used as evidence of the latter phenomenon. Some have resulted in violent and bloody conflicts, as in the break-up of Yugoslavia, while others have had an impact on well-established democracies like the United Kingdom, where in 2007 nationalist parties came to power in Scotland (a position spectacularly consolidated in

2011) and in Wales (as junior coalition partner for four years). At the same time, however, the widely anticipated decline of the nation-state in the face of globalisation does not seem to have materialised. Neither of these characterisations is very helpful in isolation. It would be more useful to focus instead on the interrelationship between nationalism and the 'cosmopolitan challenge', used here to denote a set of trends ranging from migration and the creation of diasporas to the even wider phenomena of transnationalism, regionalisation and globalisation. Rather than argue that this challenge is fundamentally antagonistic to supposedly .

beleaguered nation-states and marginalised nationalists, In The book Nationalism in the Twenty-First Century by Claire Sutherland highlights its actual interplay with nationalism and nation-building, and the ways in which nationalist ideologies have attempted to rise to the cosmopolitan challenge. Using examples from across the world, from Estonia to Fiji, and India to the USA, it does not argue that either nationalist ideology or the nation-state are in decline, but looks instead at how they are adapting to the cosmopolitan challenge.

Interpreting the principle of national self-determination to mean different degrees of autonomy, or sovereignty, is one pragmatic response to the evolution of globalisation and regional governance. Contemporary sub-state nationalists in the likes of Scotland and Catalonia also use the process of regional integration to support demands for greater autonomy from their overarching nation-states. This is just one example of how nation-states and nationalist movements are responding to the current political context, which is different to that faced by nineteenth and even twentieth-century nationalists. Regionalisation, in turn, is one among a range of contemporary phenomena which can be broadly termed the cosmopolitan challenge, and which exist in creative tension with both sub-state nationalism and nation-building. There are no clear principles regulating the relationship between globalisation, regionalisation and nationalism. Regionalisation and globalisation have been variously interpreted as beneficial or detrimental, not only to each other, but also to nation-states and nationalism more generally. If we follow the zero-sum analysis epitomised in so-called 'Eurosceptic' discourse, namely that member states 'lose' sovereignty as European integration progresses, then regionalisation appears to work against both the survival of nation-states and the aspirations of sub-state nationalists for autonomy. On the other hand, a look beyond the European Union at other forms of regional integration suggests that regionalisation does not necessarily entail a loss of sovereignty. For example, organisations like the Association of Southeast Asian Nations (ASEAN) and the North American Free Trade Area (NAFTA) are premised on intergovernmental cooperation, which does not mean ceding sovereignty, but rather aims to enhance domestic legitimacy, national prosperity and international clout.

Globalisation denotes an increase in the speed and impact of cultural, technological, economic and financial flows that is qualitatively different in scale to the important global exchanges taking place in centuries past through trade and tribute, colonialism and cultural links. With regard to the interplay between globalisation and nationalism, both phenomena are also much too wide-ranging to detect either a positive or negative correlation between the two. Some nationalists will rail against globalisation's alleged dilution of their culture and traditions. Others will point to the way in which globalisation can bring prosperity and thereby support both nation-building and nationalist appeals for greater autonomy. One useful way of approaching specific cases is to distinguish between globalisation as a macro-level phenomenon on the one hand and globalism, understood as an ideological response to that phenomenon, on the other. This separates the multifaceted process of globalisation from the political project of globalisation, there by enabling a clearer assessment of their respective relationships to nationalism.

Phenomena like regionalisation and globalisation, together with migration, transnationalism and diaspora, give a sense of the scale of the cosmopolitan challenge. The multidimensional impact of the cosmopolitan challenge on many individuals is what makes our present era qualitatively different from myriad international exchanges, which went on in past centuries. Cosmopolitanism is therefore used deliberately as an analytical concept with global scope, as opposed to the more limited, cross-border links evoked by the terms 'international' and 'transnational'. Evidently, the cosmopolitan challenge by no means affects all individuals directly or uniformly, but it definitely has the potential to influence an identity that many hold dear, namely national identity. Population flows, for instance, have an impact on existing nation-states by shaping perceptions of the national community and its members' sense of belonging. In response, nation-builders may reconfigure or entrench official markers of inclusiveness through migration and citizenship policies, as well as political discourse. Sub-state nationalists react to this by putting forward alternative understandings of nationhood and self-determination. In so doing, they are debating and defining what constitutes the nation. This is important because the current challenge to nationalists and nation-builders is to do this in a way that takes account of and even co-opts aspects of globalisation, regionalisation, transnationalism, migration and diaspora. My book looks at how different manifestations of nationalism and nation-building have responded to each of these phenomena in turn. It concludes that nationalism remains an eminently flexible ideology, which enables it to adapt to the demands of twenty-first-century politics. The cosmopolitan challenge is not insurmountable for contemporary nationalism. On the contrary, it forms part of the story of nationalism's continuing development.

TYPES OF NATIONALISM

Nationalism , as a political , social ,economic and ideological movement is characterized as many types, Many more new forms of it keeps emerging .. Most prominent ones are :

Ethnic Nationalism

Ethnic nationalism defines the nation in terms of ethnicity, which always includes some element of descent from previous generations . It also includes ideas of a culture shared between members of the group and with their ancestors, and usually a shared language. Membership in the nation is hereditary. The state derives political legitimacy from its status as homeland of the ethnic group, and from its duty to protect of the partly national group and facilitate its family and social life, as a group.

Ideas of ethnicity are very old, but modern ethnic nationalism was heavily influenced by the german nationalists Johann Gottfried von Herder and Johann Gottlieb Fichte. Theorist Anthony D. Smith uses the term 'ethnic nationalism' for non-Western concepts of nationalism, as opposed to Western views of a nation defined by its geographical territory. The term "ethno-nationalism " is generally used only in reference to nationalists who espouse an explicit ideology along these lines; "ethnic nationalism" is the more generic term, and used for nationalists who hold these beliefs in an informal, instinctive, or unsystematic way. The pejorative form of both is "ethnocentric nationalism" or "tribal nationalism," though "tribal nationalism" can have a non-pejorative meaning when discussing African, Native American, or other nationalisms that openly assert a tribal identity.

Ethnic nationalism, also known as ethno-nationalism, is a form of nationalism wherein the nation is defined in terms of ethnicity.The central theme of ethnic nationalists is that "nations are defined by a shared heritage, which usually includes a common language, a common faith, and a common ethnic ancestry".It also includes ideas of a culture shared between members of the group, and with their ancestors.

While some types of ethnic nationalism are firmly rooted in the idea of ethnicity (or race) as an immutable inherited characteristic (for example white nationalism), often ethnic nationalism also manifests in the assimilation of minority ethnic groups into the dominant group (for example as with

Italianisation). This assimilation may or may not be predicated on a belief in some common ancestry with assimilated groups (for example with Germanisation in the Second World war).

While in some cases the division between ethnic and civic nationalism is clear (France being the archetypal example of a national identity rooted in civic and linguistic nationalism), in other cases the division is less clear, for example with Turkish nationalism.

The central political tenet of ethnic nationalism is that ethnic groups can be identified unambiguously, and that each such group is entitled to self-determination.The outcome of this right to self-determination may vary, from calls for self-regulated administrative bodies within an already-established society, to an autonomous entity separate from that society, to a sovereign state removed from that society. In international relations, it also leads to policies andmovements for irredentism to claim a common nation based upon ethnicity.

In research studies , ethnic nationalism is usually contrasted with civic nationalism. Ethnic nationalism bases membership of the nation on descent or heredity, often articulated in terms of common blood or kinship, rather than on political membership. Hence, nation-states with strong traditions of ethnic nationalism tend to define nationality or citizenship by the law of blood, descent from a person of that nationality and countries with strong traditions of civic nationalism tend to define nationality or citizenship by the law of the land , birth within the nation state. Ethnic nationalism is, therefore, seen as exclusive, while civic nationalism tends to be inclusive. Rather than allegiance to common civic ideals and cultural traditions, then, ethnic nationalism tends to emphasise narratives of common descent.

The theorist Anthony D. Smith uses the term "ethnic nationalism" for non-Western concepts of nationalism as opposed to Western views of a nation defined by its geographical territory. Diaspora studies scholars extend this non-geographically bound concept of "nation" among Diaspora communities, at times using the term ethno-nation or ethno-nationalism to describe a conceptual collective of dispersed ethnics.

Ethnic nationalism is also present in many states' immigration policies in the form of repatriation laws. States such as Armenia, Bulgaria, Croatia, Estonia,

Finland, Germany, Greece, Hungary, Ireland, Israel, Italy, Malaysia, Romania, Russia, Serbia, and Turkey provide automatic or rapid citizenship to members of diasporas of their own dominant ethnic group, if desired.

In Malaysia, the Bumiputra principle recognises the "special position" of the Malays provided in the Constitution of Malaysia, in particular Article 153. However, the constitution does not use the term bumiputra; it defines only "Malay" and "indigenous peoples" (Article 160(2)), "natives" of Sarawak (161A(6)(a)), and "natives" of Sabah (Article 161A(6)(b)). Certain but not all pro-bumiputra policies exist as affirmative action for bumiputras, for NEP is racial-based and not deprivation-based. For instance, all Bumiputra, regardless of their financial standing, are entitled 7 percent discount on houses or property, including luxurious units; whilst a low-income non-Bumiputra receives no such financial assistance. Other preferential policies include quotas for the following: admission to government educational institutions, qualification for public scholarships, marking of universities exam papers, special bumiputras-only classes prior to university's end of term exams, for positions in government, and ownership of businesses. Most of the policies were established in the Malaysian New Economic Policy

(NEP) period. Many policies focus on trying to achieve a bumiputra share of corporate equity, comprising at least 30% of the total. Ismail Abdul Rahman proposed this target after the government was unable to agree on a suitable policy goal.

In German nationality law, citizenship is open to ethnic Germans. According to the Greek nationality law, Greeks born abroad may transmit citizenship to their children from generation to generation indefinitely. As of 2013 this is also true in the case of the Philippine nationality law which, has conferred Philippine citizenship on children born after 15 October 1986, with at least one Philippine citizen parent.On the other hand, civic nationalism defines membership as an individual's duty to observe given laws and in turn receive legal privileges.A nation-state for the ethnic group derives political legitimacy from its status as homeland of that ethnic group, from its protective function against colonisation, persecution, or racism, and from its claim to facilitate the shared cultural and social life, which may not have been possible under the ethnic group's previous status as an ethnic minority.

Civic Nationalism

Civic nationalism, also known as liberal nationalism, is a form of nationalism identified by political philosophers who believe in an inclusive form of nationalism that adheres with traditional liberal values of freedom, tolerance, equality, and individual rights.Civic nationalists often defend the value of national identity by saying that individuals need a national identity in order to lead meaningful, autonomous lives and that democratic polities need national identity in order to function properly.Civic nationalism is frequently contrasted with ethnic nationalism.

Civic nationalism is the form of nationalism in which the state derives political legitimacy from the active participation of its citizenry, from the degree to which it represents the "will of the people". It is often seen as originating with Jean-Jacques Rousseau and especially the social contract theories which take their name from his 1762 book The Social Contract. Civic nationalism lies within the traditions of rationalism and liberalism, but as a form of nationalism it is contrasted with ethnic nationalism. Membership of the civic nation is considered voluntary. Civic-national ideals influenced the development of representative democracy in countries such as the United States, and France.

State nationalism is a variant of civic nationalism, often combined with ethnic nationalism. It implies that the nation is a community of those who contribute to the maintenance and strength of the state, and that the individual exists to contribute to this goal. Italian fascism is the best example, epitomised in this slogan of Benito Mussolini: "Tutto nello Stato, niente al di fuori dello Stato, nulla contro lo Stato." ("Everything in the State, nothing outside the State, nothing against the State"). It is no surprise that this conflicts with liberal ideals of individual liberty, and with liberal-democratic principles. The revolutionary Jacobin creation of a unitary and centralist French state is often seen as the original version of state nationalism. Francoist Spain is a later example of state nationalism.

However, the term "state nationalism" is often used in conflicts between nationalisms, and especially where a secessionist movement confronts an established "nation state." The secessionists speak of state nationalism to discredit the legitimacy of the larger state, since state nationalism is perceived as less authentic and less democratic. Flemish separatists speak of Belgian nationalism as a state nationalism. Basque separatists and Corsican separatists refer to Spain and France, respectively, in this way. There are no undisputed external criteria to assess which side is right, and the result is usually that the population is divided by conflicting appeals to its loyalty and patriotism.

Critiques of supposed "civic nationalism" often call for the elimination of the term, as it often represents either imperialism (in the case of France), patriotism, or simply an extension of "ethnic," or "real" nationalism.

Civic nationhood is a political identity built around shared citizenship within the state. Thus, a "civic nation" isn't defined by its language or culture, but by its political institutions and liberal principles, which its citizens pledge to uphold. Membership in the civic nation is open to anyone who shares these values.

In theory, a civic nation or state does not aim to promote one culture over another. German philosopher Jürgen Habermas argued that immigrants to a liberal-democratic state need not assimilate into the host culture, but only need to accept the principles of the country's constitution

Civic nationalism lies within the traditions of rationalism and liberalism, but as a form of nationalism it is contrasted with ethnic nationalism. Membership of the civic nation is considered voluntary and the "will to live together". Civic-nationalism ideals influenced the development of representative democracy in countries such as the United States and France .The Corsican nationalist movement organised around the National liberation front of Corsica has given a civic definition of the Corsican nation ("destiny community") in the continuity of Pasquale Paoli and the ideas of the movement like Lumières (Enlighteners)

The Scottish National Party and Plaid Cymru, which advocate independence of their respective nations from the United Kingdom, proclaim themselves to be civic nationalist parties, in which they advocate the independence and popular sovereignty of the people living in their nation's society, not individual ethnic groups.The Republican Left of Catalonia supports a civic Catalan independentism and defends a Catalan Republic based on republicanism and civic values within a diverse society.

The Union of Cypriots define its ideology as Cypriot nationalism, a civic nationalism that focuses on the shared identity of Greek Cypriots and Turkish Cypriots. It highlights both communities' common culture, heritage and traditions as well as economic, political, and social rights. It also supports the reunification of Cyprus and the end of foreign interference by Greece, Turkey, and the United Kingdom.Outside Europe, it has also been used to describe the Civil War-era and Republican Party in the United States.

Expansionist Nationalism

expansionist nationalism is an aggressive and radical form of nationalism that incorporates autonomous, patriotic sentiments with a belief in expansionism. The term was coined during the late nineteenth century as European powers indulged in colonisation of Africa and parts of Asia in the name of national glory, but has been most associated with militarist governments during the twenty'th century including Fascist Italy, Nazi Germany, the Japanese empire, and the Balkans countries of Albania (Greater Albania), Bulgaria (Greater Bulgaria), Croatia (Greater Croatia), Hungary (Greater Hungary), Romania (Greater Romania) and Serbia (Greater Serbia).

What distinguishes expansionist nationalism from liberal nationalism is its acceptance of chauvinism, a belief in superiority or dominance. Nations are thus not thought to be equal to their right to self-determination; rather some nations are believed to possess characteristics or qualities that make them superior to others. Expansionist nationalism therefore asserts the state's right to increase its borders at the expense of it's neighbours .

What distinguishes expansionist nationalism from liberal nationalism is its acceptance of chauvinism, a belief in superiority or dominance. Nations are thus not thought to be equal to their right to self-determination; rather some nations are believed to possess characteristics or qualities that make them superior to others. Expansionist nationalism therefore asserts the state's right to increase its borders at the expense of its neighbours.

Expansionist nationalism is opposed to all aspects of liberal nationalism. Most notably, expansionist nationalism rejects the right to national self-determination.

Expansionist nationalism is also opposed to inclusion, diversity and social progress. Expansionist nationalism is characterised by the mindset of chauvinism and the language of jingoism. This belligerent stance towards others is at times employed by political leaders who identify the inherent advantages of creating and identifying a scapegoat.

Expansionist nationalism is clearly an extreme form of nationalism, and ultra-nationalism is a core element of fascist ideology. There are many fascist organisations throughout the history of the world that have utilised the language of expansionist nationalism to serve their own ends. That said, in the contemporary era the influence of fascist organisations is relegated to the margins of the political process.

The only comparable movement that carries any global significance is that of Islamo-fascism, a term coined by the French philosopher Michel Onfray shortly after the 1979 Iranian Revolution. Like other fascist movements throughout history; Islamo-fascism promises certainty in a world of uncertainty, a sense of unity with others and an appealing message to those who feel that their world-view is the one true path we must all follow. It has its scapegoats (Zionism and its Western allies), its slogans ('remaining and expanding'), its moral and messianic rhetoric, its search for breathing space in the form of a caliphate and its treatment of women as second-class citizens ,all backed up by its doctrinaire followers. Such observations could equally apply to those who supported or sympathised with the Nazis during the 1920-1930's and some of the ultra nationalist leaders of modern times and their followers trying almost same rhetoric to grab power.

DS KARTIKA

Organic Nationalism

Organic nationalism is the form of nationalism in which the state derives its political legitimacy as an organic consequence of the unity of those it governs.This includes, depending on the particular manner of practice, the language, race, culture, religion, and customs of the nation in its primal sense of those who were born within its culture. This form of nationalism arose in reaction to dynastic or imperial hegemony, which assessed the legitimacy of the state from the top down, emanating from a monarch or other authority, which justified its existence. Some scholars refers this type of nationalism as romantic Nationalism or National romanticism or Identity Nationalism as well.

Among the key themes of Romanticism, and its most enduring legacy, the cultural assertions of romantic nationalism have also been central in post-Enlightenment art and political philosophy. From its earliest stirrings, with their focus on the development of national languages and folklore, and the spiritual value of local customs and traditions, to the movements that would redraw the map of Europe and lead to calls for self-determination of nationalities, nationalism was one of the key issues in Romanticism, determining its roles, expressions and meanings.

Historically in Europe, the watershed year for romantic nationalism was 1848, when a revolutionary wave spread across the continent; numerous nationalistic revolutions occurred in various fragmented regions (such as Italy) or multinational states (such as the Austrian Empire). While initially the revolutions fell to reactionary forces and the old order was quickly re-established, the many revolutions would mark the first step towards liberalisation and the formation of modern nation states across much of Europe.

Linguistic and cultural nationality, coloured with pre-genetic concepts of race, bolstered two rhetorical claims consistently associated with romantic nationalism to this day such as claims of primacy and claims of superiority. Primacy is the claimed inalienable right of a culturally and racially defined people to a geographical terrain, a "heartland" or homeland. The polemics of racial superiority became inexorably intertwined with romantic nationalism. Richard Wagner notoriously argued that those who were ethnically different could not comprehend the artistic and cultural meaning inherent in national culture. Identifying "Jewishness" even in musical style, he specifically attacked the Jews as being unwilling to assimilate into German culture, and thus unable to truly comprehend the mysteries of its music and language. Sometimes "national epics" such as the Nibelungenlied have had a galvanizing effect on social politics.

In the first two decades of the 20th century, Romantic Nationalism as an idea was to have crucial influence on political events. Following the Panic of 1873 that gave rise to a new wave of anti-Semitism and racism in the German Empire politically ruled by an authoritarian, militaristic conservatism under Otto von Bismarck and in parallel with a wide revival of irrational emotionalism known as Fin de siècle (also reflected to a degree in the contemporary art movements of symbolism, the Decadent movement, and Art Nouveau), the racist, so-called volkisch movement grew out of Romantic nationalism during the last third of the 19th century, to some extent modelling itself on British Imperialism and "the White Man's Burden". The idea was that Germans should "naturally" rule over lesser peoples. Romantic nationalism, which had begun as a revolt against "foreign" kings and overlords, had come full circle, and was being used to make the case for a "Greater Germanic Empire" which would rule over Europe.

The nationalistic and imperialistic tensions rising high between the European nations throughout the irrational, neo-romantic Fin de siècle period eventually erupted in the First World War. After Germany had lost the war and undergone the tumultuous German Revolution, the volkisch movement drastically radicalised itself in Weimar Germany under the harsh terms of the Treaty of Versailles, and Adolf Hitler would go on to say that "the basic ideas of National-Socialism are volkisch, just as the volkisch ideas are National-Socialist".

Outside of Germany, the belief among European powers was that nation-states forming around unities of language, culture and ethnicity were "natural" in some sense. For this reason President Woodrow Wilson would argue for the creation of self-determining states in the wake of the Great War. However, the belief in romantic nationalism would be honoured in the breach. In redrawing the map of Europe, Yugoslavia was created as an intentional coalition state among competing, and often mutually hostile, southern Slavic peoples, and the League of Nations' mandates were often drawn, not to unify ethnic groups, but to divide them. To take one example, the nation now known as Iraq intentionally joined together three Ottoman vilayets, uniting

Kurds in the north, Sunni Arabs in the centre, and Shia Arabs in the south, in an effort to present a strong national buffer state between Turkey and Persia: over these was placed a foreign king from the Hashemite dynasty native to the Hijaz.

Because of the broad range of expressions of romantic nationalism, it is listed as a contributing factor from everything from the creation of independent states in Europe, to the rise of Nazi Germany. As an idea, if not a specific movement, it is present as an assumption in debates over nationality and nationhood even today, and many of the world's nations were created from principles drawn from romantic nationalism as their source of legitimacy.

Cultural Nationalism

Cultural nationalism has been described as a variety of nationalism that is neither purely civic nor ethnic.Cultural nationalism" does not tend to manifest itself in independent movements, but is a moderate position within a larger spectrum of nationalist ideology.Cultural nationalism defines the nation by shared culture. Membership in the nation is neither entirely voluntary, nor hereditary .Children of members may be considered foreigners if they grew up in another culture. Yet, a traditional culture can be more easily incorporated into an individual's life, especially if the individual is allowed to acquire its skills at an early stage of his or her own life.

Cultural nationalism encompasses the feelings of cultural pride that people have in a society. This society is typically an ethnically diverse makeup of people who have common cultural beliefs and a common language but not a common race or ancestry. An "ethnically diverse" society usually defined as one with multiple ethnic groups that each comprise a substantial percentage of the population. These societies thus have a shared culture even when they do not share the historically common characteristics of a national group. These characteristics mainly being race and ethnicity, the way groups have typically been separated throughout history. Hence, the ideas and feelings of cultural nationalism are built upon shared cultural ideals and norms among a society. These shared ideals and norms may include political ideologies, recognition of holidays, a specific and unique cuisine, etc. The other main idea of cultural nationalism is the shared language of the groups of people. While societies that are ethnically and racially homogeneous usually also share a common language, culturally nationalistic societies typically have a common language and different races of people who also speak a native language from a previous society or country along with that common language.

As previously stated, feelings of cultural nationalism are not limited to ethnically diverse societies, although it is more common and much easier to define as different ethnicities co-existing with each other in such societies create a cultural umbrella. People in an ethnically homogeneous society may feel pride for the society's political ideologies, for example, but not care for or identify feelings of pride towards the common ethnicity of that society, giving a technical definition of cultural nationalism.

The history of cultural nationalism throughout the world tends to be more prevalent in modern and contemporary history, i.e. late 19th century to the present. This is the case because before this time, societies that included multiple ethnic groups were typically not unified culturally. Since the early empires of ancient Rome and Greece in which diverse groups were under the control of one governing body, many conquered peoples retained their own culture and traditions. Their use under the governing body was mainly for labor, taxation, soldiers, etc. Some empires such as the British, created systems in conquered and occupied lands to specifically avoid sharing of culture, such as segregation of races, limited access to certain works of literature, etc. Empires, many of which didn't collapse until World War I, were limited in their ability to brew cultural nationalism because even with the great many ethnic groups, a unified culture wasn't typically sought after, the ethnic groups usually being seen as opportunities for diversity of labor and resources instead of culture.

Cultural nationalism thus relies on integration of differing ethnic groups, a lot of which didn't happen until the mid-twentieth century. Civil rights movements in the mid-twentieth century gave ethnic and racial groups in multiracial societies more of the same rights as their other peers in society, giving more unity and thus more of a shared culture instead of a separated one. This integration isn't limited to separate races, gender and women's movements were very key in the twentieth century as many advancements in the rights for women such as suffrage in 1920 in the United States, and equal pay midway through the century. Segregation and separation are great deterrents to unified cultural nationalism as it perpetuates certain groups fighting for different things, creating disunity. Many systemic segregation and separation policies did not end until the mid to late twentieth century in many parts of the world, especially in the West, where cultural nationalism is the strongest presently.

Cultural nationalism has seen its heaviest increase in the late twentieth century as many totalitarian regimes and nations have fallen, giving way for people to move freely throughout the world and migrate and diversify other societies. The fall of the Soviet Union for example in the early 1990s allowed for millions of people to leave the previously blocked in "Iron Curtain" and move to western nations, adopting the culture of the new nation, as many disagreed with the culture of their communist Soviet state.

During this time in the last quarter of the twentieth century there were also many waves of immigration from Asia and South America to western nations, especially the United States, where American culture was adopted typically quickly by many of these immigrant groups.

While cultural nationalism is present in many areas of the world, Western cultures are where it is the most prevalent. While some western nations and societies, especially those in Europe, have just recently acquired demographics and culture that constitutes growth of cultural nationalism, some societies such as those of the United States were founded on principles of cultural nationalism that have remained and strengthened to this day.

Western nations normally experience stronger sentiments of cultural nationalism due to the high levels of diversity in these nations. Immigration to these nations from typically more impoverished or dangerous nations is widespread due to many of the common open-door policies of Western nations to accept a certain number of immigrants, refugees, students, etc. These immigrants who are generally grateful for the ability to settle in these nations typically adopt the culture of their new nation, mixing with their own heritage, and typically conforming more and more to their new nation's culture as new generations are born in that nation.

According to its proponents, one benefit of cultural nationalism is racial unification- in a typical culturally nationalistic society that has multiple racial groups all living in the same society, race tends to be less of an importance in dominant culture. Although there are still many racial divides throughout such nations for many reasons, the general idea of cultural nationalism puts the shared nationality of multiple races at the forefront, thus letting, for example, a black soldier fight along a white soldier, or a black president have a white vice president, etc., thus unifying different races in many instances.

Post -Colonial Nationalism

In most countries that experienced some form of direct colonial rule Nationalism emerged as a political and intellectual movement embraced by a broad spectrum of social elites . Nationalist leaders varying backgrounds shared a common interest in extricating the nation from colonial rule and in establishing an independent nation state with a distinct , unified national identity .In most cases however the common bond that had been crafted during the course of the independence movement was subsequently challenged by divisive tendencies , some new and some historically entrenched ,after national independence was achieved .

Since the process of decolonisation that occurred after World War II, there has been a rise of Third World nationalisms. Third world nationalisms occur in those nations that have been colonised and exploited. The nationalisms of these nations were forged in a furnace that required resistance to colonial domination in order to survive. As such, resistance is part and parcel of such nationalisms and their very existence is a form of resistance to imperialist intrusions. Third World nationalism attempts to ensure that the identities of Third World peoples are authored primarily by themselves, not colonial powers and that's what post colonial nationalism is all about.

Examples of third world nationalist ideologies are African nationalism and Arab nationalism. Other important nationalist movements in the developing world have included Indian nationalism, Chinese nationalism and the ideas of the Mexican Revolution and Haitian Revolution. Third world nationalist ideas have been particularly influential among the raft of left-leaning governments elected in South America in recent years, particularly on President of Venezuela Hugo Chavez's ideology of Bolivarianism which has been partly inspired by the anti-colonial ideals of Simon Bolivar.

Liberation Nationalism

Many nationalist movements in the world are dedicated to national liberation, in the view that their nations are being persecuted by other nations and thus need to exercise self-determination by liberating themselves from the accused persecutors. Anti-revisionist Marxist–Leninism is closely tied with this ideology, and practical examples include Stalin's early work Marxism and the National Question and his Socialism in One Country edict, which declares that nationalism can be used in an internationalist context i.e. fighting for national liberation without racial or religious divisions.

Wars of national liberation or national liberation revolutions are conflicts fought by nations to gain independence. The term is used in conjunction with wars against foreign powers (or at least those perceived as foreign) to establish separate sovereign states for the rebelling nationality. From a different point of view, these wars are called insurgencies, rebellions, or wars of independence. Guerrilla warfare or asymmetric warfare is often utilized by groups labeled as national liberation movements, often with support from other states.

The term "wars of national liberation" is most commonly used for those fought during the decolonisation movement. Since these were primarily in the third world against Western powers and their economic influence and a major aspect of the Cold War, the phrase itself has often been viewed as biased or pejorative.[2] Some of these wars were either vocally or materially supported by the Soviet Union, which stated itself to be an anti-imperialist power, supporting the replacement of western-backed governments with local communist or other non pro-western parties.

However, this did not always guarantee Soviet influence in those countries. In addition to and increasingly in competition to the Soviet Union, the People's Republic of China presented themselves as models of independent nationalist development outside of Western influence, particularly as such posturing and other long term hostility meant they were regarded as a threat to Western power and regarded themselves as such, using their resources to politically, economically and militarily assist movements such as in Vietnam. In January 1961 Soviet premier Nikita Khrushchev pledged support for" wars of national liberation" throughout the world.

Socialist Nationalism

Socialist Nationalism , very much a twentieth-century phenomenon, is of far more recent origin than other types. Usually motivated by a concern to protect achievements accomplished or reach goals pursued in national politics, socialist nationalism has at some time or other been directed against every form of internationalism, including some socialist varieties. It has been mainly reactive and defensive.

Socialist Nationalism also known as left-wing nationalism refers to any political movement that combines left-wing politics with nationalism. Notable examples include Fidel Castro's 26th of July Movement that launched the Cuban Revolution ousting the American-backed Fulgencio Batista in 1959, Ireland's Sinn Fein, Labor Zionism in Israel and the African National Congress in South Africa.

Conservative Nationalism

Conservative Nationalism is a political term used primarily in Europe to describe a variant of conservatism which concentrates more on national interests than standard conservatism, while not being nationalist or a far-right approach. Many national conservatives are social conservatives, in favour of limiting immigration, and in Europe, they usually are eurosceptics.Also known as National conservatism, is related to social conservatism, and as such may be heavily oriented towards the traditional family and social stability.

GLOBALISATION & NATIONALISM VS PATRIOTISM

Anarchists Nationalism

Anarchists who see value in nationalism typically argue that a nation is first and foremost a people; that the state is parasite upon the nation and should not be confused with it; and that since in reality states rarely coincide with national entities, the ideal of the Nation State is actually little more than a myth. Within the European Union, for instance, they argue there are over 500 ethnic nations within the 25 member states, and even more in Asia, Africa, and the Americas. Moving from this position, they argue that the achievement of meaningful self-determination for all of the worlds nations requires an anarchist political system based on local control, free federation, and mutual aid. There has been a long history of anarchist involvement with left-nationalism all over the world. Contemporary fusions of anarchism with anti-state left-Nationalism include some strains of Black anarchism and Indigenism.

In the early to mid 19th century Europe, the ideas of nationalism, socialism, and liberalism were closely intertwined. Revolutionaries and radicals like Giuseppe Mazzini aligned with all three in about equal measure.The early pioneers of anarchism participated in the spirit of their times: they had much in common with both liberals and socialists, and they shared much of the outlook of early nationalism as well. Thus Mikhail Bakunin had a long career as a pan-Slavic nationalist before adopting anarchism. He also agitated for a United States of Europe (a contemporary nationalist vision originated by Mazzini).In 1880-1881, the Boston-based Irish nationalist W. G. H. Smart wrote articles for a magazine called The Anarchist. Similarly, Anarchists in China during the early part of the 20th century were very much involved in the left-wing of the nationalist movement while actively opposing racist elements of the Anti-Manchu wing of that movement.

Pan Nationalism

Pan-nationalism is a form of nationalism distinguished by being associated with a claimed national territory which does not correspond to existing political boundaries. It often defines the nation as a "cluster" of closely related ethnic or cultural groups. It shares the general nationalist premises that the nation is a fundamental unit of human social life, and that it is the only legitimate basis for the state

Diaspora Nationalism

Diaspora nationalism (or, as Benedict Anderson terms it, "long-distance nationalism") generally refers to nationalist feeling among a diaspora such as the Irish in the United States, Jews around the world after the expulsion from Jerusalem (586 BCE), the Lebanese in the Americas and Africa, or Armenians in Europe and the United States. Anderson states that this sort of nationalism acts as a "phantom bedrock" for people who want to experience a national connection, but who do not actually want to leave their diaspora community. The essential difference between pan-nationalism and diaspora nationalism is that members of a diaspora, by definition, are no longer resident in their national or ethnic homeland. Traditionally 'Diaspora' refers to a dispersal of a people from a (real or imagined) 'homeland' due to a cataclysmic disruption, such as war, famine, etc. New networks - new 'roots' - form along the 'routes' travelled by Diaspora people, who are connected by a shared desire to return 'home'. In reality, the desire to return may be eschatological or may not occur in any foreseeable future, but the longing for the lost homeland and the sense of difference from circumambient cultures in which Diaspora people live becomes an identity unto itself.

Right-wing Nationalism

Religious nationalism is the relationship of nationalism to a particular religious belief, church, or affiliation. This relationship can be broken down into two aspects; the politicisation of religion and the converse influence of religion on politics. In the former aspect, a shared religion can be seen to contribute to a sense of national unity, a common bond among the citizens of the nation. Another political aspect of religion is the support of a national identity, similar to a shared ethnicity, language or culture. The influence of religion on politics is more ideological, where current interpretations of religious ideas inspire political activism and action, for example, laws are passed to foster stricter religious adherence.

Economic Nationalism

Economic nationalism is a form of nationalism that specifically prioritises domestic businesses. It seeks to defend them against multinational corporations that benefit from globalism. It advocates protectionism and other trade policies that protect local industries. President Trump espoused economic nationalism when he announced tariffs on steel and Chinese imports.

Economic nationalism also prefers bilateral trade agreements between two countries. It says that multilateral agreements benefit corporations at the expense of individual nations. It would even adopt unilateral agreements where the stronger nation forces a weaker nation to adopt trade policies that favour the stronger country.

The policies were proven to fail during the Great Depression. After the stock market crash of 1929, countries began adopting protectionist measures in a desperate attempt to save jobs. Instead, it sent the world economy down, plummeting 65 percent. As a result, those measures prolonged the depression.

To compensate for less trade, economic nationalism advocates increased fiscal policies to help businesses. This includes increased government spending on infrastructure and tax cuts for businesses.

Economic nationalism opposes immigration because it takes jobs away from domestic workers. Trump's immigration policies followed nationalism when he promised to build a wall on the border with Mexico.

PATRIOTISM

PATRIOTISM

What is patriotism ? How is it related to similar attitudes, such as nationalism and its importance in the age of globalisation ? What is its moral standing? Is it morally valuable or perhaps even mandatory, or is it rather a stance we should avoid? Yet until a few decades ago, philosophers used to show next to no interest in the subject. The article on patriotism in the Historical Dictionary of Philosophy, reviewing the use of the term from the 16th century to our own times, gives numerous references, but they are mostly to authors who were not philosophers. Moreover, of the few well known philosophers cited, only one, J. G. Fichte, gave the subject more than a passing reference and most of what Fichte had to say actually pertains to nationalism, rather than patriotism

This changed in the 1980s. The change was due, in part, to the revival of communitarianism, which came in response to the individualistic, liberal political and moral philosophy epitomised by John Rawls' theory of justice but it was also due to the resurgence of nationalism in several parts of the world.

The beginning of this change was marked by Andrew Oldenquist's account of morality as a matter of various loyalties, rather than abstract principles and ideals , and Alasdair MacIntyre's argument that patriotism is a central moral virtue . Largely in response to MacIntyre, some philosophers have defended constrained or deflated versions of patriotism . Others have argued against patriotism of any sort .

There is now a lively philosophical debate about the moral credentials of patriotism that shows no signs of abating. A parallel discussion in political philosophy concerns the kind of patriotism that might provide an alternative to nationalism as the ethos of a stable, well-functioning polity.

Discussions of both patriotism and nationalism are often marred by lack of clarity due to the failure to distinguish the two. Many authors use the two terms interchangeably. Among those who do not, quite a few have made the distinction in ways that are not very helpful. In the 19th century, Lord Acton contrasted "nationality" and patriotism as affection and instinct vs. a moral relation.

Nationality is "our connection with the race" that is "merely natural or physical," while patriotism is the awareness of our moral duties to the political community . In the 20th century, Elie Kedourie did the opposite, presenting nationalism as a full-fledged philosophical and political doctrine about nations as basic units of humanity within which the individual can find freedom and fulfilment, and patriotism as mere sentiment of affection for one's country.

George Orwell contrasted the two in terms of aggressive vs. defensive attitudes. Nationalism is about power, its adherent wants to acquire as much power and prestige as possible for his nation, in which he submerges his individuality. While nationalism is accordingly aggressive, patriotism is defensive, it is a devotion to a particular place and a way of life one thinks best, but has no wish to impose on others .

This way of distinguishing the two attitudes comes close to an approach popular among politicians and widespread in everyday discourse that indicates a double standard of the form "us vs. them." Country and nation are first run together and then patriotism and nationalism are distinguished in terms of the strength of the love and special concern one feels for it, the degree of one's identification with it. When these are exhibited in a reasonable degree and without ill thoughts about others and hostile actions towards them, that is patriotism, when they become unbridled and cause one to think ill of others and act badly towards them, that is nationalism. Conveniently enough, it usually turns out that we are patriots, while they are nationalists .

There is yet another way of distinguishing patriotism and nationalism ,one that is quite simple and begs no moral questions. We can put aside the political sense of "nation" that makes it identical with "country," "state," or "polity," and the political or civic type of nationalism related to it. We need to concern ourselves only with the other, ethnic or cultural sense of "nation," and focus on ethnic or cultural nationalism. In order to do so, we do not have to spell out the relevant understanding of "nation", it is enough to characterise it in terms of common ancestry, history, and a set of cultural traits. Both patriotism and nationalism involve love , identification with and special concern for a certain entity. In the case of patriotism, that entity is one's patria, one's country, in the case of nationalism, that entity is one's natio, one's nation (in the ethnic/cultural sense of the term). Thus patriotism and nationalism are understood as the same type of set of beliefs and attitudes, and distinguished in terms of their objects, rather than the strength of those beliefs and attitudes, or as sentiment vs. theory.

To be sure, there is much overlap between country and nation, and therefore between patriotism and nationalism. Thus much of that applies to one ,will also apply to the other. But when a country is not ethnically homogeneous, or when a nation lacks a country of its own, the two may part ways.

Patriotism has had a fair number of critics. The harshest among them have judged it deeply flawed in every important respect. In the 19th century, Russian novelist and thinker Leo Tolstoy found patriotism both stupid and immoral. It is stupid because every patriot holds his own country to be the best of all whereas, obviously, only one country can qualify. It is immoral because it enjoins us to promote our country's interests at the expense of all other countries and by any means, including war, and is thus at odds with the most basic rule of morality, which tells us not to do to others what we would not want them to do to us . Recently, Tolstoy's critique has been seconded by American political theorist George Kateb, who argues that patriotism is "a mistake twice over, it is typically a grave moral error and its source is typically a state of mental confusion" .

Patriotism is most importantly expressed in a readiness to die and to kill for one's country. But a country "is not a discernible collection of discernible individuals"; it is rather "an abstraction, a compound of a few actual and many imaginary ingredients." Specifically, in addition to being a delimited territory, "it is also constructed out of transmitted memories true and false, a history usually mostly falsely sanitised or falsely heroised , a sense of kinship of a largely invented purity and social ties that are largely invisible or impersonal, indeed abstract ..." Therefore patriotism is "a readiness to die and to kill for an abstraction , for what is largely a figment of the imagination"

Some of these objections can easily be countered. Even if full-fledged patriotism does involve a belief in one's country's merits, it need not involve the belief that one's country is better than all others. And the fact that a country is not a collection of "discernible individuals" and that the social ties among compatriots are "largely invisible or impersonal," rather than palpable and face-to-face, does not show that it is unreal or imaginary. As

Benedict Anderson, who coined the term "imagined community," points out, "all communities larger than primordial villages of face-to-face contact are imagined." "Imagined community" is not the opposite of "real community," but rather a community whose members have face-to-face relations .

However, there is another, more plausible line of criticism of patriotism focusing on its intellectual, rather than moral credentials. Moreover, Tolstoy's and Kateb's arguments questioning the moral legitimacy of patriotic partiality and those highlighting the connection of patriotism with international tensions and war cannot be so easily refuted.

Ethics of patriotism

When asked "why do you love your country?" or "why are you loyal to it?", a patriot is likely to take the question to mean "what is so good about your country that you should love it, or be loyal to it?" and then adduce what she believes to be its virtues and achievements. This suggests that patriotism can be judged from the standpoint of ethics of belief – a set of norms for evaluating our beliefs and other doxastic attitude. Simon Keller has examined patriotism from this point of view, and found it wanting.

Keller argues that whereas one's love of and loyalty to a family member or a friend may coexist with a low estimate of the person's qualities, patriotism involves endorsement of one's country. If the patriot is to endorse her country, she must consider her beliefs about the country's virtues and achievements to be based on some objectively valid standards of value and an unbiased examination of the country's past and present record that leads to the conclusion that it lives up to those standards.

However, the patriot's loyalty is not focused on her country simply because it instantiates a set of virtues a country can have. If that were the case, and if a neighbouring country turned out to have such virtues to an even higher degree, the patriot's loyalty would be redirected accordingly. She is loyal to her country because that country, and only that country, is her country; hers is a loyalty "in the first instance." Thus the patriot is motivated to think of the patria as blessed by all manner of virtues and achievements whether the evidence, interpreted objectively, warrants that or not. Accordingly, she forms beliefs about her country in ways different from the ways in which she forms beliefs about other countries. Moreover, she cannot admit this motivation while at the same time remaining a patriot. This leads her to hide from herself the true source of some of the beliefs involved. This is bad faith. Bad faith is bad ,so is patriotism, as well as every identity, individual or collective, constituted, in part, by patriotic loyalty. This, in Keller's view, amounts to "a clear presumptive case against patriotism's being a virtue and for its being a vice" .

This portrayal does seem accurate as far as much patriotism as we know it, is concerned. Yet Keller may be overstating his case as one against patriotism as such. When queried about one's loyalty to one's country, couldn't one say: "This is my country, my home; I need no further reason to be loyal to it and show special concern for its well-being"? This might not be a very satisfactory answer; we might agree with J.B. Zimmermann that "the love for one's country is in many cases no more than the love of an ass for its stall" . But however egocentric, irrational, asinine, surely it qualifies as patriotism. Keller seems to be of two minds on this point.

Many think of patriotism as a natural and appropriate expression of attachment to the country in which we were born and raised and of gratitude for the benefits of life on its soil, among its people, and under its laws. They also consider patriotism an important component of our identity. Some go further, and argue that patriotism is morally mandatory, or even that it is the core of morality. There is, however, a major tradition in moral philosophy which understands morality as essentially universal and impartial, and seems to rule out local, partial attachment and loyalty. Adherents of this tradition tend to think of patriotism as a type of group egoism , a morally arbitrary partiality to "one's own" at odds with demands of universal justice and common human solidarity. A related objection is that patriotism is exclusive in invidious and dangerous ways. Love of one's own country characteristically goes together with dislike and hostility towards other countries. It tends to encourage militarism, and makes for international tension and conflict. Tolstoy's and Kateb's moral objections to patriotism, mentioned above, are in line with this position. What, then, is the moral status of patriotism? The question does not admit of a single answer.

Types of patriotism

We can distinguish five types of patriotism and each needs to be judged on its merits.

Extreme patriotism

Machiavelli is famous or infamous for teaching princes that, human nature being what it is, if they propose to do their job well, they must be willing to break their promises, to deceive, dissemble, and use violence, sometimes in cruel ways and on a large scale, when political circumstances require such actions. This may or may not be relevant to the question of patriotism, depending on just what we take the point of princely rule to be. A less well known part of Machiavelli's teaching, however, is relevant, for he sought to impart the same lesson to politicians and common citizens of a republic. "When the safety of one's country wholly depends on the decision to be taken, no attention should be paid either to justice or injustice, to kindness or cruelty, or to its being praiseworthy or ignominious" The paramount interests of one's country override any moral consideration with which they might come into conflict.

This type of patriotism is extreme, but by no means extremely rare. It is adopted much too often by politicians and common citizens alike when their country's major interests are thought to be at stake. It is encapsulated in the saying "our country, right or wrong," at least on the simplest and most obvious construal of this saying. Not much needs to be said about the moral standing of this type of patriotism, as it amounts to rejection of morality. "Our country, right or wrong" cannot be right.

Robust patriotism

In his seminal lecture "Is Patriotism a Virtue?" Alasdair MacIntyre contrasts patriotism with the liberal commitment to certain universal values and principles. On the liberal view, where and from whom I learn the principles of morality is just as irrelevant to their contents and to my commitment to them, as where and from whom I learn the principles of mathematics is irrelevant to their contents and my adherence to them. For MacIntyre, where and from whom I learn my morality is of decisive importance both for my commitment to it and for its very contents.

There is no morality as such; morality is always the morality of a particular community. One can understand and internalise moral rules only "in and through the way of life of [one's] community" . Moral rules are justified in terms of certain goods they express and promote, but these goods, too, are always given as part and parcel of the way of life of a community. The individual becomes a moral agent only when informed as such by his community. He also lives and flourishes as one because he is sustained in his moral life by his community".I can only be a moral agent because we are moral agents

… Detached from my community, I will be apt to lose my hold upon all genuine standards of judgment" .

If I can live and flourish as a moral agent only as a member of my community, while playing the role this membership involves, then my very identity is bound up with that of my community, its history, traditions, institutions, and aspirations. Therefore,

if I do not understand the enacted narrative of my own individual life as embedded in the history of my country … I will not understand what I owe to others or what others owe to me, for what crimes of my nation I am bound to make reparation, for what benefits to my nation I am bound to feel gratitude. Understanding what is owed to and by me and understanding the history of the communities of which I am a part is … one and the same thing.

This leads MacIntyre to conclude that patriotism is not to be contrasted with morality; it is rather a central moral virtue, indeed the bedrock of morality.

The object of patriotic loyalty is one's country and polity; but this does not mean that a patriot will support any government in power in her country. Here MacIntyre's position is different from a popular version of patriotism that tends to conflate the two. The patriot's allegiance, he says, is not to the status quo of power, but rather to "the nation conceived as a project" . One can oppose one's country's government in the name of the country's true character, history, and aspirations. To that extent, this type of patriotism is critical and rational. But at least some practices and projects of the patria, some of its "large interests," must be beyond questioning and critical scrutiny. To that extent, MacIntyre grants that what he considers true patriotism is "a fundamentally irrational attitude" (13). But a more rational and therefore more constrained loyalty would be "emasculated," rather than real patriotism.

This account of patriotism is exposed to several objections. One might question the communitarian foundations of MacIntyre's case for patriotism: his view of the moral primacy of the community over the individual. One might find fault with the step from communitarianism to patriotism:

Even if his communitarian conception of morality were correct and even if the process of moral development ensured that group loyalty would emerge as a central virtue, no conclusion would follow about the importance of patriotism. The group to which our primary loyalty would be owed would be the group from which we had obtained our moral understanding. This need not be the community as a whole or any political unit, however. It could be one's family, one's town, one's religion. The nation need not be the source of morality or the primary beneficiary of our loyalty.

Yet another objection would focus on the fundamentally irrational character of robust patriotism: its insistence that "large interests" of the patria must be beyond questioning.

MacIntyre concedes that "on occasion patriotism might require me to support and work for the success of some enterprise of my nation as crucial to its overall project ... when the success of that enterprise would not be in the best interests of mankind" . If so, this type of patriotism would seem to involve the rejection of such basic moral notions as universal justice and common human solidarity.

Tolstoy and other critics have argued that patriotism is incompatible with these notions – that it is egoism writ large, an exclusive and ultimately aggressive concern for one's country, and a major cause of international tensions and war. This is not a fair objection to patriotism as such. Patriotism is defined as a special concern for one's country's well-being, and that is not the same as an exclusive and aggressive concern for it. But the objection is pertinent, and has considerable force, when brought up against the type of patriotism advocated by MacIntyre. MacIntyre's patriot may promote his country's interests in a critical, and therefore non-exclusive way, over a range of issues. But when it comes to those "large interests" of his country that are beyond criticism and must be supported in an irrational way, his concern will inevitably become exclusive, and most likely aggressive too. If justice is understood in universal, rather than parochial terms, if common human solidarity counts as a weighty moral consideration, and if peace is of paramount importance and war is morally permissible only when it is just, then this kind of patriotism must be rejected.

GLOBALISATION & NATIONALISM VS PATRIOTISM

Moderate patriotism

Rejecting robust patriotism does not entail adopting sweeping imperialism that acknowledges no special obligations, and allows no partiality, to "our own." Nor does it entail adopting the more restricted, cosmopolitan position, that allows no partiality to our own country and compatriots. There is considerable middle ground between these extremes. Exploring this middle ground has led some philosophers to construct positions accommodating both the universal and the particular point of view – both the mandates of universal justice and claims of common humanity, and the concern for the patria and compatriots.

One such position is "patriotism compatible with liberal morality," or "liberal patriotism" for short, advocated by Marcia Baron . Baron argues that the conflict between impartiality and partiality is not quite as deep as it may seem. Morality allows for both types of considerations, as they pertain to different levels of moral deliberation. At one level, we are often justified in taking into account our particular commitments and attachments, including those to our country. At another level, we can and ought to reflect on such commitments and attachments from a universal, impartial point of view, to delineate their proper scope and determine their weight. We can conclude, for example, "that with respect to certain matters and within limits, it is good for an American to judge as an American, and to put American interests first" . In such a case, partiality and particular concerns are judged to be legitimate and indeed valuable from an impartial, universal point of view. This means that with respect to those matters and within the same limits, it is also good for a Cuban to judge as a Cuban and to put Cuban interests first, etc. Actually, this is how we think of our special obligations to, and preferences for, our family, friends, or local community; this kind of partiality is legitimate, and indeed valuable, not only for us but for anyone.

In MacIntyre's view, the type of partiality in general, and patriotism in particular, that is at work only at one level of moral deliberation and against the background of impartiality at another, higher level, lacks content and weight. For Baron, on the other hand, MacIntyre's strongly particularistic type of patriotism is irrational and morally hazardous. Baron also finds problematic the popular understanding of patriotism which focuses on the country's might and its interests as determined by whatever government is in power. She emphasises concern for the country's cultural and moral excellence. By doing so, she argues, our patriotism will leave room for serious, even radical criticism of our country, and will not be a force for dissension and conflict in the international arena.

Another middle-of-the-road view is "moderate patriotism" propounded by Stephen Nathanson . He, too, rejects the choice between MacIntyre's robust patriotism and cosmopolitanism, and argues that impartiality required by morality allows for particular attachments and special obligations by distinguishing different levels of moral thinking. A good example is provided by the Ten Commandments, a major document of Western morality. The wording of the commandments is for the most part universal, impartial, but they also tell us "honour your father and your mother."

The kind of patriotism defended by Nathanson and Baron is moderate in several distinct, but related respects. It is not unbridled: it does not enjoin the patriot to promote his country's interests under any circumstances and by any means. It acknowledges the constraints morality imposes on the pursuit of our individual and collective goals. For instance, it may require the patriot to fight for his country, but only in so far as the war is, and remains, just.

Adherents of both extreme and robust patriotism will consider themselves bound to fight for their country whether its cause be just or not. Extreme patriots will also fight for it in whatever way it takes to win. Whether adherents of MacIntyre's robust patriotism, too, will do so is a moot point. If they do not, that will be because the morality of their own community places certain constraints on warfare, whether of a particularistic type or by incorporating some universalistic moral precepts .

Moderate patriotism is not exclusive. Its adherent will show special concern for his country and compatriots, but that will not prevent him from showing concern for other countries and their inhabitants. Moreover, this kind of patriotism allows for the possibility that under certain circumstances the concern for human beings in general will override the concern for one's country and compatriots. Such patriotism is compatible with a decent degree of humanitarianism. By contrast, both extreme and robust patriotism give greater weight to the interests of one's country and compatriots than to those of other countries and their inhabitants whenever these interests come into conflict.

Finally, moderate patriotism is not uncritical, unconditional, or egocentric. For an adherent of this type of patriotism, it is not enough that the country is her country. She will also expect it to live up to certain standards and thereby deserve her support, devotion and special concern for its well-being. When it fails to do so, she will withhold support. Adherents of both extreme and robust patriotism, on the other hand, love their country unconditionally, and stand by it whatever it does as long as its "safety" or its "large interests" more generally are concerned.

Baron and Nathanson have found a middle ground between sweeping cosmopolitanism that allows for no attachment and loyalty to one's country and compatriots, and extreme or robust patriotism that rejects universal moral considerations ,except those that have become part and parcel of one's country's morality. They have shown that the main objections usually advanced against patriotism as such apply only to its extreme or robust varieties, but not to its "liberal" or "moderate" versions. The latter type of patriotism need not conflict with impartial justice or common human solidarity. It will therefore be judged morally unobjectionable by all except some adherents of a strict type of cosmopolitanism.

However, both Baron and Nathanson fail to distinguish clearly between showing that their preferred type of patriotism is morally unobjectionable and showing that it is morally required or virtuous, and sometimes seem to be assuming that by showing the former, they are also showing the latter. Yet there is a gap between the two claims, and the latter, stronger case for moderate patriotism still needs to be made.

Deflated Patriotism

What is the case for the claim that moderate patriotism is morally mandatory that we have a duty of special concern for the well-being of our country and compatriots, similar to special duties to family or friends?

Gratitude is probably the most popular among the grounds adduced for patriotic duty. Echoing Socrates in Plato's Crito , Maurizio Viroli writes: "We have a moral obligation towards our country because we are indebted to it. We owe our country our life, our education, our language, and, in the most fortunate cases, our liberty. If we want to be moral persons, we must return what we have received, at least in part, by serving the common good" .

Both Socrates and Viroli are exaggerating the benefits bestowed on us by our country , surely any gratitude owed for being born or brought up is owed to parents, rather than patria. But there are important benefits we have received from our country; the argument is that we are bound to show gratitude for them, and that the appropriate way to do so is to show special concern for the well-being of the country and compatriots.

DS KARTIKA

One worry here is that considerations of gratitude normally arise in interpersonal relations. We also speak of gratitude to large and impersonal entities – our school, profession, or even our country – but that seems to be an abbreviated way of referring to gratitude to particular persons who have acted on behalf of these entities. A debt of gratitude is not incurred by any benefit received. If a benefit is conferred inadvertently, or advisedly but for the wrong reason (e.g. for the sake of the benefactor's public image), gratitude will be misplaced. We owe a moral debt of gratitude (rather than the mere "thank you" of good manners) only to those who confer benefits on us deliberately and for the right reason, namely out of concern for our own good. And we cannot talk with confidence about the reasons a large and complex group or institution has for its actions.

Perhaps we can think of compatriots as an aggregate of individuals. Do we owe them a debt of gratitude for the benefits of life among them? Again, it depends on the reason for their law-abiding behaviour and social cooperation generally. But there is no single reason common to all or even most of them. Some do their part without giving much thought to the reasons for doing so; others believe that doing so is, in the long run, the most prudent policy; still others act out of altruistic motives. Only the last group – surely a tiny minority – would be a proper object of our gratitude.

Moreover, gratitude is appropriate only for a benefit conferred freely, as a gift, and not as a quid pro quo. But most of the benefits we receive from our country are of the latter sort , benefits we have paid for ,by our own law-abiding behaviour in general and through taxation in particular.

The benefits one has received from her country might be considered relevant to the duty of patriotism in a different way: as raising the issue of fairness. One's country is not a land inhabited by strangers to whom we owe nothing beyond what we owe to any other human being. It is rather a common enterprise that produces and distributes a wide range of benefits. These benefits are made possible by cooperation of those who live in the country, participate in the enterprise, owe and render allegiance to the polity. The rules that regulate the cooperation and determine the distribution of burdens and benefits enjoin, among other things, special concern for the well-being of compatriots which is not due to outsiders. As Richard Dagger puts it:

Compatriots take priority because we owe it to them as a matter of reciprocity. Everyone, compatriot or not, has a claim to our respect and concern … but those who join with us in cooperative enterprises have a claim to special recognition. Their cooperation enables us to enjoy the benefits of the enterprise, and fairness demands that we reciprocate. … We must accord our fellow citizens a special status, a priority over those who stand outside the special relationship constituted by the political enterprise. Our fellow citizens have a claim on us … that extends to include the notion that compatriots take priority.

This argument conflates the issue of patriotism with that of political obligation and the notion of a patriot with that of a citizen. Unlike informal cooperation among tenants in a building, for instance, cooperation on the scale of a country is regulated by a set of laws. To do one's part within such a cooperative enterprise is just to obey the laws, to act as a citizen. Whether we have a moral duty to obey the laws of our country is one of the central issues in modern political philosophy, discussed under the heading of political obligation. One major account of political obligation is that of fairness. If successful, that account shows that we do have a moral duty to abide by the laws of our country, to act as citizens, and that this duty is one of fairness. To fail to abide by one's country's laws is to fail to reciprocate, to take advantage of compatriots, to act unfairly towards them. But whereas a patriot is also a citizen, a citizen is not necessarily a patriot. Patriotism involves special concern for the patria and compatriots, a concern that goes beyond what the laws obligate one to do, beyond what one does as a citizen; that is, beyond what one ought, in fairness, to do. Failing to show that concern, however, cannot be unfair – except on the question-begging assumption that, in addition to state law, cooperation on this scale is also based on, and regulated by, a moral rule enjoining special concern for the well-being of the country and compatriots. Dagger asserts that the claim our compatriots have on us "extends to include" such concern, but provides no argument in support of this extension.

Some philosophers seek to ground patriotic duty in its good consequences . The duty of special concern for the well-being of our country and compatriots, just like other duties, universal and special, is justified by the good consequences of its adoption. Special duties mediate our fundamental, universal duties and make possible their most effective discharge. They establish a division of moral labor, necessary because our capacity of doing good is limited by our resources and circumstances. Each of us can normally be of greater assistance to those who are in some way close to us than to those who are not. By attending first to "our own," we at the same time promote the good of humanity in the best way possible.

Patriots will find this account of their love of and loyalty to their country alien to what they feel patriotism is all about. It presents the duty of special concern for the well-being of one's country and compatriots as a device for assigning to individuals some universal duties. Patriotic duty owes its moral force to the moral force of those universal duties. But if so, then, as a proponent of this understanding of patriotism concedes, "It turns out that 'our fellow countrymen' are not so very special after all" . They merely happen to be the beneficiaries of the most effective way of putting into practice our concern for human beings in general. The special relationship between the patriot and the patria and compatriots – the relationship of love and identification – has been dissolved.

There is also a view of patriotic duty that, in contrast to the consequentialist account, does not dissolve, but rather highlight this relationship. That is the view of patriotism as an associative duty (see the entry on special obligations ,section 4). It is based on an understanding of special relationships as intrinsically valuable and involving duties of special concern for the well-being of those we are related to. Such duties are not means of creating or maintaining those relationships, but rather their part and parcel, and can only be understood, and justified, as such, just as those relationships can only be understood as involving the special duties pertaining to them (while involving much else besides). For instance, one who denies that she has an obligation of special concern for the well-being of her friend shows that she no longer perceives and treats the person concerned as a friend, that (as far as she is concerned) the friendship is gone. One who denies that people in general have a duty of special concern for the well-being of their friends shows that she does not understand what friendship is.

Andrew Mason has offered an argument for the duty of special concern for the well-being of compatriots based on the value embodied in our relationship to compatriots, that of common citizenship. By "citizenship" he does not mean mere legal status, but takes the term in a moral sense, which involves equal standing. Citizenship in this sense is an intrinsically valuable relationship, and grounds certain special duties fellow citizens have to one another. Now citizenship obviously has considerable instrumental value; but how is it valuable in itself?

Citizenship has intrinsic value because in virtue of being a citizen a person is a member of a collective body in which they enjoy equal status with its other members and are thereby provided with recognition. This collective body exercises significant control over its members' conditions of existence (a degree of control which none of its members individually possesses). It offers them the opportunity to contribute to the cultural environment in which its laws and policies are determined, and opportunities to participate directly and indirectly in the formation of these laws and policies.

Mason goes on to claim that Part of what it is to be a citizen is to incur special obligations: these obligations give content to what it is to be committed or loyal fellow citizen and are justified by the good of the wider relationship to which they contribute. In particular, citizens have an obligation to each other to participate fully in public life and an obligation to give priority to the needs of fellow citizens.

The first of these two special duties can be put aside, as it is not specific to patriotism, but rather pertains to citizenship. It is the second that is at issue. If we indeed have a duty of special concern towards compatriots, and if that is an associative duty, that is because our association with them is intrinsically valuable and bound up with this duty. The claim about the intrinsic value of our association might be thought a moot point. But even if it were conceded, one might still resist the claim concerning the alleged duty. If someone were to deny that she has a duty of special concern for the well-being of her country and compatriots, beyond what the laws of her country mandate and beyond the concern she has for humans and humanity, would she thereby cease to be a citizen (in the sense involving equal standing)? If she were to deny that citizens generally have such an obligation, would that betray lack of understanding of what citizenship (in the relevant sense) is? If she came across two strangers in a life-threatening situation and could only save one, would she have a prima facie moral duty to save the one who was a compatriot? Mason's position commits him to answering "yes" in each case, but all three claims are implausible .

All the main arguments for the claim that patriotism is a duty, then, are exposed to serious objections.

Unless a new, more convincing case for patriotism can be made, we have no good reason to think that patriotism is a moral duty. If not a duty, is patriotism morally valuable? Someone showing concern for the well-being of others well beyond the degree of concern for others required of all of us is considered a morally better person than the rest of us (other things equal), an example of supererogatory virtue.

Patriotism is a special concern for the well-being of one's country and compatriots, a concern beyond what we owe other people and communities. Isn't a patriot, then, a morally better person than the rest of us ? Isn't patriotism a supererogatory virtue?

One standard example of such virtue is the type of concern for those in an extreme plight shown by the late Mother Theresa, or by Doctors Without Borders. But they are exemplars of moral virtue for the same reason that makes a more modest degree of concern for others a moral duty falling on all of us. The same moral value, sympathy for and assistance to people in need, grounds a certain degree of concern for others as a general moral duty and explains why a significantly higher degree of such concern is a moral ideal.

This explanation, however, does not apply in the case of patriotism. Patriotism is not but another extension of the duty of concern for others; it is a special concern for my country because it is my country, for my compatriots because they are my compatriots. Unlike Mother Theresa and Doctors Without Borders, whose concern is for all destitute, sick, dying persons they can reach, the concern of the patriot is by definition selective and the selection is performed by the word "my." But the word "my" cannot, by itself, play the critical role in an argument showing that a certain stance is morally valuable. If it could, other types of partialism, such as tribalism, racism, or sexism, would by the same token prove morally valuable too.

If patriotism is neither a moral duty nor a supererogatory virtue, then all its moral pretensions have been deflated. It has no positive moral significance. There is nothing to be said for it, morally speaking. We all have various preferences for places and people, tend to identify with many groups, large and small, to think of them as in some sense ours, and to show a degree of special concern for their members. But however important in other respects these preferences, identifications, and concerns might be, they lack positive moral import. They are morally permissible as long as they are kept within certain limits, but morally indifferent in themselves. The same is true of patriotism.

Ethical patriotism

All four types of patriotism reviewed so far seek to defend and promote what might be termed the worldly (non-moral, interests of the patria, its political stability, military power, riches, influence in the international arena, and cultural vibrancy. They differ with regard to the lengths to which these interests will be promoted: adherents of extreme and robust patriotism will ultimately go to any length, whereas those whose patriotism is moderate or deflated will respect the limits universal moral considerations set to this pursuit. Marcia Baron also calls for expanding patriotic concern for the flourishing of one's country to include its "moral flourishing"

Thus Baron's position is half-way between the usual, worldly kind of patriotism, and what might be described as its distinctively ethical type. The latter would put aside the country's well-being in a mundane, non-moral sense, and would focus instead on its distinctively moral well-being, its moral identity and integrity. A patriot of this sort would not express his love for the patria by seeking to husband the country's resources and preserve its natural beauty and its historical heritage, or make it rich, powerful, culturally preeminent, or influential on the world scene. Instead, he would seek to make sure that the country lives up to moral requirements and promotes moral values, both at home and internationally. He would work for a just and humane society at home, and seek to ensure that the country acts justly beyond its borders, and shows common human solidarity towards those in need, however distant and unfamiliar. He would also be concerned with the country's past moral record and its implications for the present. He would support projects exploring the dark chapters of the country's history, acknowledging the wrongs perpetrated in the past and responding to them in appropriate ways, whether by offering apologies or making amends, and by making sure such wrongs are not perpetrated again.

A patriot of this, distinctively ethical type, would want to see justice done, rights respected, human solidarity at work at any time and in any place. But her patriotism would be at work in a concern that her country be guided by these moral principles and values which is more sustained and more deeply felt than her concern that these principles and values should be put into practice generally. She would consider her own moral identity as bound up with that of her country, and the moral record of the patria as hers too. Unlike a patriot of the more worldly type, she might not feel great pride in her country's worldly merits and achievements. She would be proud of the country's moral record, when it inspires pride. But her patriotism would be expressed, above all, in a critical approach to her country and compatriots: she would feel entitled, and indeed called, to submit them to critical moral scrutiny, and to do so qua patriot.

While we have no moral reason to be patriots of the more usual, mundane kind, we do have reason to show special concern for our own country's moral well-being. As a rule, when someone is wronged, someone else benefits from that. When a country maintains an unjust or inhumane practice, or enacts and enforces an unjust or inhumane law or policy, at least some, and sometimes many of its citizens reap benefits from it. Sometimes such a practice, legislation or policy affects people beyond the country's borders; in such cases, the population as a whole may benefit. The responsibility for the injustice or lack of basic human solidarity lies with those who make the decisions and those who implement them. It also lies with those who give support to such decisions and their implementation. But some responsibility in this connection may also devolve on those who have no part in the making of the decisions or in their implementation, nor even provide support, but accept the benefits such a practice, law or policy generates.

A degree of complicity may also accrue to those who have no part in designing or putting into effect immoral practices, laws or policies, do not support them or benefit from them, but do benefit in various ways from being citizens of the country. One may derive significant psychological benefit from membership in and identification with a society or polity: from the sense of belonging, support and security such membership and identification afford. If one accepts such benefits, while knowing about the immoral practices, laws or policies at issue, or having no excuse for not knowing about them, that, too, may be seen as implicating him in those wrongs. To be sure, he makes no causal contribution to those wrongdoings, has no control over their course, and does not accept benefits from them. But in accepting benefits from his association with the wrongdoers, he may be seen as underwriting those wrongs and joining the class of those properly blamed. His complicity is lesser and the blame to be laid at his door is lesser too – but he still bears some moral responsibility and deserves some moral blame on that account. He cannot say in good faith: "Those wrongs have nothing to do with me. I am in no way implicated in them."

If this is correct, we have reason to develop and exercise a special concern for the moral identity and integrity of our country. By doing so, we will be attending to an important aspect of our own moral identity and integrity. While patriotism of the more usual, worldly kind is neither morally required nor virtuous, but at best morally permitted, ethical patriotism can, under certain fairly common circumstances, be a moral duty.

Role of patriotism

While moral philosophers debate the standing of patriotism as an instance of the problem of reconciling universal moral considerations with particular attachments and loyalties, political theorists are primarily interested in patriotism as an ethos of the well-ordered polity and an antidote to nationalism. Since the rise of the nation-state, it has been widely held that some form of nationalism is indispensable as a pre-political basis of the unity of the state that makes for solidarity among citizens and provides them with motivation to participate in public life and make sacrifices for the common good.

As Roger Scruton put it, "for a liberal state to be secure, the citizens must understand the national interest as something other than the interest of the state. Only the first can evoke in them the sacrificial spirit upon which the second depends" . But in the course of the 20th century, nationalism was deeply compromised. That has led political theorists to look for alternatives. Some have argued that an emphatically political patriotism could perform the unifying function of nationalism while avoiding its perils. This "new patriotism" puts aside, or at least de-emphasises, pre-political ties such as common ancestry, language, or culture, and enjoins love of, and loyalty to, one's political community, its laws and institutions, and the rights and liberties they make possible.

In view of the disastrous record of national socialism, it is not surprising that German thinkers in particular should be suspicious of patriotism as long as it has not been dissociated from nationalism. As early as 1959, political theorist Dolf Sternberger called for a new understanding of the concept of fatherland. "The fatherland is the 'republic,' which we create for ourselves. The fatherland is the constitution, to which we give life. The fatherland is the freedom which we truly enjoy only when we ourselves promote it, make use of it, and stand guard over it". In 1979, on the 30th anniversary of the Federal Republic, he coined the term "constitutional .patriotism" to describe the loyalty to the patria understood in these terms . The term was later adopted by Jürgen Habermas in the context of a case for overcoming pre-political, i.e. national and cultural, loyalties in public life, and supplanting them with a new, post-national, purely political identity embodied in the laws and institutions of a free and democratic state. Habermas argues that this identity, expressed in and reinforced by constitutional patriotism, can provide a solid foundation for such a state, given the ethnic and cultural heterogeneity characteristic of most countries in western Europe. It can also facilitate further European integration, and provide an antidote to the "chauvinism of affluence" tempting these countries.

Constitutional patriotism is the most widely discussed, but not the sole variety of "new patriotism." Another is "covenanted patriotism" advocated by John H. Schaar as appropriate for countries whose population is much too ethnically and culturally heterogeneous to allow for "natural patriotism." Schaar's paradigmatic example is the United States, whose citizens "were bonded together not by blood or religion, not by tradition or territory, not by the walls and traditions of a city, but by a political idea by a covenant, by dedication to a set of principles and by an exchange of promises to uphold and advance certain commitments" . Still another variety is the "patriotism of liberty" propounded by Maurizio Viroli, who calls for a return to what patriotism used to be before it was harnessed in the service of the nation-state and submerged in nationalism: love of the laws and institutions of one's polity and the common liberty they make possible .

This new, emphatically political version of patriotism has been met with both sympathy and skepticism. Those sympathetic to it have been discussing the prospects of a European constitutional patriotism . Skeptics have argued that patriotism disconnected from all pre-political attachments and identities can generate only much too thin a sense of identity and much too weak a motivation for political participation – that, thus understood, "patriotism is not enough"

Differences of Patriotism and Nationalism

Patriotism is love of country and devotion to the welfare of compatriots with a passion which inspires to serve the country unlike the Nationalism which desire to compete with other nations.The two are often confused and frequently believed to mean the same thing. However, there is a vast difference between nationalism and patriotism. Nationalism is a feeling that one's country is superior to another in all respects, while patriotism is merely a feeling of admiration for a way of life in a country.

The difference between patriotism and nationalism is simple , a patriot loves his country and is proud of it for what it does whereas a nationalist loves his country and is proud of his country no matter what it does .The first attitude creates a feeling of responsibility but the second a feeling of blind arrogance that leads to conflicts .

Nationalism must be distinguished from patriotism. Patriotism is fundamental to liberty because pride in one's nation-state, and a willingness to defend it, if necessary, is the basis of national independence. Patriotism is the courage of national self-determination.

DS KARTIKA

By contrast, nationalism is patriotism transformed into a sentiment of superiority and aggression toward other countries. Nationalism is the poisonous idea that one's country is superior to somebody else's or everybody else's.Nationalism is intrinsically a cause of conflicts and imperialism.

Nationalist and Globalist versus patriotism

Given their fundamental disagreements over human nature and the moral value of parochialism, it is inevitable that Globalists and Nationalists would disagree about the moral value of patriotism.Most definitions of patriotism refer to positive feelings about one's country (love, devotion, pride) and a sense of duty or obligation to support or protect it. Patriotism is therefore a form of parochialism—it is a commitment to a local and circumscribed group instead of adopting a Global or "citizen of the

world" identity. This is why Globalists are often critical of patriotism and why they sometimes say things about patriotism or criticises their country that Nationalists perceive it to be disloyal at best, and treasonous at worst.

When a country is attacked by a foreign enemy, there is almost always a surge of patriotism. People have a strong urge to come together and many of them reach for the flag. Americans saw this happen after the Japanese attack on Pearl Harbor, and again after the Al Qaeda attacks of September 11, 2001. Britain saw this happen at the start of both World Wars, and again after the Al Qaeda attacks on the London transport system in 2005. In the wake of those terrorist attacks, British intellectuals debated whether some form of patriotism was compatible with progressivism.

George Monbiot, a leading thinker of the British left, took a strong position against the moral value of patriotism. In an essay titled "The New Chauvinism," Monbiot rejected what he called "an emerging national consensus," which included some left-of-centre writers, that what they need in Britain was a renewed sense of patriotism.Monbiot granted that a widely shared sense of patriotism might make British citizens (including Muslim citizens) less likely to attack each other, but he made the good counter-point that patriotism makes the state more inclined to attack other countries as it knows it is likely to command the support of its people.

If patriotism were not such a powerful force in the United States, could Bush have invaded Iraq?Monbiot then asserted that "Globalist or Internationalist should use a strictly utilitarian framework to resolve moral questions because internationalists believe that all lives are of equal worth. He then argued that from this utilitarian perspective, patriotism is almost always unethical.

When confronted with a conflict between the interests of your country and those of another, patriotism, by definition demands that you should choose those of your own. Internationalism (globalism) by contrast, means choosing the option which delivers most good or least harm to people, regardless of where they live. It tells us that someone living in Kinshasa is of no less worth than someone living in Kensington, and that a policy which favours the interests of 100 British people at the expense of 101 Congolese is one we should not pursue. Patriotism, if it means anything, tells us we should favour the interests of the 100 British people. How do you reconcile this choice with liberalism? How, for that matter, do you distinguish it from racism? This is the kind of statement that turns many people away from Globalism.

Most people believe that that their own government should place their welfare above that of foreigners, just as most people believe that their own spouse, mother, friend, boss, or teammate should care more about them than about a stranger far away. The willingness to erase local loyalties and obligations in order to maximize overall utility makes sense in John Lennon's imaginary world, but it is sacrilege from a Durkheimian perspective in which people have distinctive duties tied to their particular roles and relationships. And if Burke and Smith are correct, then universalism won't even deliver the benefits in reality that it promises in the abstract.

To be a nationalist, in America or in Europe, is to be frequently lectured to and called a rube by the globalist elite. The globalists assert things to be obvious and indisputable facts like the strength of diversity ,that seem to nationalists to be obvious and indisputable falsehoods. The globalists explain away the nationalists' policy preferences as resulting both from lack of education and from selfishness ,for example not wanting immigrants taking scarce resources from the National Health Service. The globalists assemble panels of economists and other academics, and sometimes even movie stars, to argue their case. This is why Brexit leader Michael Gove said, "I think people in this country have had enough of experts." This is why Donald Trump's attacks on "political correctness" have won him the gratitude of so many working-class and rural white voters. Even if you are a globalist, can you see why nationalists are often full of seething resentment? Can you see why people who feel a deep emotional attachment to their country and want to preserve its sovereignty and culture are angry at people ,who tell them that they are wrong to do so?So let us take another look at patriotism. Are there forms that might be acceptable to both globalists and to nationalists?

As the conflict between globalists and nationalists has moved to centre stage in many countries in recent times , several commentators have offered insightful new thinking about patriotism and nationalism. The key question all have addressed is that how can people show love and loyalty to their nation in ways that bring benefits to their nation while minimising the harm done both to immigrants within the country and to citizens of other countries?

The economist Larry Summers responded to the Brexit vote with an article titled: "Voters Deserve Responsible Nationalism not Reflex Globalism." As an economist who is firmly convinced of the value of international trade, he acknowledged that big trade agreements, such as NAFTA, have often failed to live up to the hype that had been used to sell them to voters. He noted that "the willingness of people to be intimidated by experts into supporting cosmopolitan outcomes appears for the moment to have been exhausted." He urged Western nations to adopt a new approach that directly rejects Monbiot's universalism.

A new approach has to start from the idea that the basic responsibility of government is to maximise the welfare of citizens, not to pursue some abstract concept of the global good.What is needed is a responsible nationalism.An approach where it is understood that countries are expected to pursue their citizen's economic welfare as a primary objective but where their ability to harm the interests of citizens elsewhere is circumscribed. International agreements would be judged not by how much is harmonised or by how many barriers are torn down but whether citizens are empowered.

Examining immigration rather than trade, the philosopher David Miller just published a book with the timely title 'Strangers in Our Midst'.Like Summers, he concludes that states do have special duties to care for their own citizens, even as they attempt to act humanely toward others. In the end he recommends that the immigration policies of liberal democracies be guided by four values such as weak cosmopolitanism, national self-determination, fairness, and social integration. By "weak cosmopolitanism" he means a broadly humanitarian orientation in which "we must always consider the effects of our actions on all those who will bear the consequences, no matter who they are or whether they are in any way connected to us," yet at the same time, he believes we are not obligated to treat the claims and interests of non-citizens as equal to those of citizens. Miller specifically rejects as overly demanding and unrealistic a "strong cosmopolitanism" in which all human beings have equal claim on each nation's care, protection and money.

And finally, New York Times columnist David Brooks wrote a column about the Globalist-Nationalist debate titled "We Take Care of Our Own."He summarised 'my American Interest essay ' and then improved upon it by showing how America in particular can easily formulate a patriotism acceptable to both sides. He notes that America, unlike most other countries, was founded as a universalist nation. It has long been a source of pride that America takes people from many countries and unites them behind American ideals. Like Stenner, Brooks criticises "the forces of multiculturalism" for damaging America's longstanding commitment to cultural union and assimilation. This damage left an opening, he says, for Donald Trump's unwelcoming nationalism, which has more in common with the kind of "European blood and soil" nationalism that is often overtly racist.

Brooks concludes that the way out of this debate is not to go nationalist or globalist. It's to return to

American nationalism espoused by people like Walt Whitman, which combines an inclusive definition of who is Our Own with a fervent commitment to assimilate and Take Care of them.Brooks' essay was published on July 15, 2016, six days before Donald Trump gave his acceptance speech at the Republican National Convention in which he painted a dark vision of America going to hell in a dangerous world.Trump's nationalism was all about "us" versus "them" and how we can kick them out or otherwise defeat them. It was the opposite of Brooks' recommendation; it was what Summers would call "irresponsible nationalism."

The Democrats, in contrast, in their convention, did exactly what Brooks urged. It is to be expected that the Democrats would feature speakers from all races, each waving the American flag symbolically or literally; that's normal convention showmanship. But for many viewers, the emotional highlight of the week occurred on Thursday, July 28, 2016, just before Hillary Clinton was introduced by her daughter, Chelsea. The speaker before Chelsea was Khizr Khan, an immigrant from Pakistan whose son Humayun joined the U S. Army and fought in Iraq. Humayun died a hero's death, having stepped forward to intercept an approaching car loaded with explosives. He saved the soldiers under his command and possibly many more on the base they were guarding. His father addressed the convention and the country:Tonight we are honoured to stand here as parents of Captain Humayun Khan and as patriotic American Muslims with undivided loyalty to our country. Like many immigrants, we came to this country empty-handed. We believed in American democracy, that with hard work and goodness of this country, we could share in and contribute to its blessings.Then, directly addressing his remarks to Donald Trump, who had said he would try to restrict Muslim immigration to America.Let me ask you Mr. Trump, have you even read the United States constitution? I will gladly lend you my copy ,He pulls out his copy from his jacket pocket and continues, in this document, look for the words "liberty" and "equal protection of law." Have you ever been to Arlington Cemetery? Go look at the graves of brave patriots who died defending the United States of America. You will see all faiths, genders, and ethnicities. You have sacrificed nothing and no one.Khan's embrace of America, its values, and its constitution was a stirring example of a kind of patriotism that can unite most nationalists and most globalists. It celebrates "us" without denigrating "them." It is welcoming and assimilationist.

This approach may not work in countries that define themselves by the history of a single ethnic group. But with some tinkering it should work in Britain ,which can take credit for having pioneered so many liberal institutions. In France ,whose revolution was one of ideas and rights and in other countries that have long traditions of openness, or of taking in refugees.

Diversity is difficult and often divisive. It's not shades of skin colour that divides, it is the perception that people in other groups have different values and that they behave in ways that violate our moral worldview. Among the most important divisions within many Western nations is now the division between globalists and nationalists. The two sides have many real differences that must be worked out by a long and difficult political process. But political disagreements may become more tractable if both sides can understand each other a little better, and if both sides share a love of their country that is both passionate and to varying degrees, perhaps welcoming .

Politics of globalisation ,nationalism and patriotism

In an era of Globalisation ,the new fault line in politics, according to Marine Le Pen, leader of France's far-right National Front, is between globalists and patriots. It is an argument similar to those being made by eurosceptics in the United Kingdom and Republican president Donald Trump in the United States. It is, however, as false as it is dangerous.Judging by the results ,French voters, at least, roundly rejected it. They cast 73 percent of their ballots for the National Front's rivals.

Le Pen accused the mainstream parties of ganging up on her, describing their cooperation as a denial of democracy. Her argument is, of course, a classic example of sour grapes , the entire point of a two-round voting system is to force parties and their supporters to seek a consensus and form partnerships.

Le Pen statement that those who vote for her party are the only true patriots was casually dismissed. She has homed in on a powerful message, one with the potential to attract supporters from other parties. That's why it must be rebutted, both in France and elsewhere. The assumption underlying such nationalist bombast that a country's interests are better served by being closed rather than open is extremely dangerous.

The belief that openness is treason and closure is patriotic is a rejection of the entire post-1945 framework of politics and policy in the developed world. It is an attempt to turn back the clock to the interwar period, when the focus was on closing off, imposing onerous trade restrictions and persecuting or expelling minority groups. This was true even in the U.S., which enacted the most restrictive immigration laws since the country's founding.

The postwar years marked a complete change of direction, as countries opened up, allowing freer flows of trade, capital, ideas, and people. This process became known as globalisation only after China and India joined in during the 1980s, but it had started long before. It was globalisation, after all, that created what in France became known as Les Trente Glorieuses — the 30 glorious years of rapidly rising living standards following the end of World War II.

Le Pen and her fellow populists claim that globalisation was either an act of foolish generosity that helped the rest of the world at the expense of the nation or a phenomenon that benefited only the elites and not ordinary people. For them, patriotism means being harder-headed about protecting the national interest and adopting more democratic policies that help the working masses, not jet-setting fat cats.

The second part of this argument that the interests of ordinary people have been subordinated to those of the elite , must be heard and responded to. A democracy in which a majority feels neglected or exploited is not sustainable. Either the government or the entire system will be overturned.Elected representatives clearly need to find answers to high unemployment and declining living standards. What mainstream parties need to be make clear, however, is that the answers to those problems do not lie in closing borders or minds. There is no example, anywhere in history, of a society or an economy that has prospered over the long term by rejecting globalisation.

Moreover, though openness may not guarantee prosperity, it has always been a prerequisite for growth. To be sure, the optimal amount of openness is a matter of debate. But the bigger, more productive arguments are about how to shape education, labor markets, scientific research and social-welfare policies in order to help societies adapt to the world around them. The patriotic choice and the national interest has always consisted in crafting domestic policies that best take advantage of globalisation.

For mainstream parties in France, the Conservatives in the United Kingdom., and Trump's more internationally minded Republican rivals in the United States , there is nothing to be gained from copying the arguments of their extremist counterparts. Doing so would yield crucial ground in the political battle over how best to serve the country and its people. Mainstream parties must reclaim the mantle of patriotism and redefine the national interest accordingly. In today's world, the national interest lies in managing openness , not in throwing it away.

AUTHOR

D S KARTIKA

www.ingramcontent.com/pod-product-compliance
Lightning Source LLC
Chambersburg PA
CBHW061347280526
45784CB00001B/165